INSTITUTE OF PACIFIC RELATIONS

INQUIRY SERIES

THE INSTITUTE OF PACIFIC RELATIONS

The Institute of Pacific Relations is an unofficial and non-political body, founded in 1925 to facilitate the scientific study of the peoples of the Pacific Area. It is composed of National Councils in eleven countries.

The Institute as such and the National Councils of which it is composed are precluded from expressing an opinion on any aspect of national or international affairs; opinions expressed in this study are, therefore, purely individual.

NATIONAL COUNCILS OF THE INSTITUTE

American Council, Institute of Pacific Relations

Australian Institute of International Affairs

Canadian Institute of International Affairs

China Institute of Pacific Relations

Comité d'Études des Problèmes du Pacifique

Japanese Council, Institute of Pacific Relations

Netherlands-Netherlands Indies Council, Institute of Pacific Relations

New Zealand Institute of International Affairs

Philippine Council, Institute of Pacific Relations

Royal Institute of International Affairs

U.S.S.R. Council, Institute of Pacific Relations

JAPAN SINCE 1931

JAPAN SINCE 1931

ITS POLITICAL AND SOCIAL DEVELOPMENTS

By

HUGH BORTON

Assistant Professor of Japanese
Columbia University

I. P. R. INQUIRY SERIES

INTERNATIONAL SECRETARIAT

INSTITUTE OF PACIFIC RELATIONS

PUBLICATIONS OFFICE, 129 EAST 52ND STREET, NEW YORK

1940

FOREWORD

This study forms part of the documentation of an Inquiry organized by the Institute of Pacific Relations into the problems arising from the conflict in the Far East.

It has been prepared by Dr. Hugh Borton, Assistant Professor of Japanese, Columbia University.

The Study has been submitted in draft to a number of authorities including the following, many of whom made suggestions and criticisms which were of great value in the process of revision: Mr. G. E. Hubbard, Mr. Nagaharu Yasuo and Dr. Charles B. Fahs.

Though many of the comments received have been incorporated in the final text, the above authorities do not of course accept responsibility for the study. The statements of fact or of opinion appearing herein do not represent the views of the Institute of Pacific Relations or of the Pacific Council or of any of the National Councils. Such statements are made on the sole responsibility of the author. The Japanese Council has not found it possible to participate in the Inquiry, and assumes, therefore, no responsibility either for its results or for its organization.

During 1938 the Inquiry was carried on under the general direction of Dr. J. W. Dafoe as Chairman of the Pacific Council and in 1939 under his successor, Dr. Philip C. Jessup. Every member of the International Secretariat has contributed to the research and editorial work in connection with the Inquiry, but special mention should be made of Mr. W. L. Holland, Miss Kate Mitchell and Miss Hilda Austern, who have carried the major share of this responsibility.

In the general conduct of this Inquiry into the problems arising from the conflict in the Far East the Institute has benefited by the counsel of the following Advisers:

Professor H. F. Angus of the University of British Columbia

Dr. J. B. Condliffe of the University of California

M. Etienne Dennery of the École des Sciences Politiques.

These Advisers have cooperated with the Chairman and the Secretary-General in an effort to insure that the publications issued in connection with the Inquiry conform to a proper standard of sound and impartial scholarship. Each manuscript has been submitted to at least two of the Advisers and although they do not necessarily subscribe to the statements or views in this or any of the studies, they consider this study to be a useful contribution to the subject of the Inquiry.

The purpose of this Inquiry is to relate unofficial scholarship to the problems arising from the present situation in the Far East. Its purpose is to provide members of the Institute in all countries and the members of I.P.R. Conferences with an impartial and constructive analysis of the situation in the Far East with a view to indicating the major issues which must be considered in any future adjustment of international relations in that area. To this end, the analysis will include an account of the economic and political conditions which produced the situation existing in July 1937, with respect to China, to Japan and to the other foreign Powers concerned; an evaluation of developments during the war period which appear to indicate important trends in the policies and programs of all the Powers in relation to the Far Eastern situation; and finally, an estimate of the principal political, economic and social conditions which may be expected in a post-war period, the possible forms of adjustment which might be applied under these conditions, and the effects of such adjustments upon the countries concerned.

The Inquiry does not propose to "document" a specific plan for dealing with the Far Eastern situation. Its aim is to focus available information on the present crisis in forms which will be useful to those who lack either the time or the expert knowledge to study the vast amount of material now appearing or already published in a number of languages. Attention may also be drawn to a series of studies on topics bearing on the Far Eastern situation which is being prepared by the Japanese Council. That series is being undertaken entirely independently of this Inquiry, and for its organization and publication the Japanese Council alone is responsible.

The present study, "Japan Since 1931," falls within the framework of the second of the four general groups of studies which it is proposed to make as follows:

I. The political and economic conditions which have contributed to the present course of the policies of Western Powers in the Far East; their territorial and economic interests; the effects on their Far Eastern policies of internal economic and political developments and of developments in their foreign policies vis-à-vis other parts of the world; the probable effects of the present conflict on their positions in the Far East; their changing attitudes and policies with respect to their future relations in that area.

II. The political and economic conditions which have contributed to the present course of Japanese foreign policy and possible important future developments; the extent to which Japan's policy toward China has been influenced by Japan's geographic conditions and material resources, by special features in the political and economic organization of Japan which directly or indirectly affect the formulation of her present foreign policy, by economic and political developments in China, by the external policies of other Powers affecting Japan; the principal political, economic and social factors which may be expected in a post-war Japan; possible and probable adjustments on the part of other nations which could aid in the solution of Japan's fundamental problems.

III. The political and economic conditions which have contributed to the present course of Chinese foreign policy and possible important future developments; Chinese unification and reconstruction, 1931-37, and steps leading toward the policy of united national resistance to Japan; the present degree of political cohesion and economic strength; effects of resistance and current developments on the position of foreign interests in China and changes in China's relations with foreign Powers; the principal political, economic and social factors which may be expected in a post-war China; possible and probable adjustments on the part of other nations which could aid in the solution of China's fundamental problems.

IV. Possible methods for the adjustment of specific problems, in the light of information and suggestions presented in the three studies outlined above; analysis of previous attempts at bilateral or multilateral adjustments of political and economic relations in the Pacific and causes of their success or failure; types of administrative procedure and controls already tried out and their relative effectiveness; the major issues likely to require international adjustment in a post-war period and the most hopeful methods which might be devised to meet them; necessary adjustments by the Powers concerned; the basic requirements of a practical system of international organization which could promote the security and peaceful development of the countries of the Pacific area.

EDWARD C. CARTER
Secretary-General

New York,
October 1, 1940

AUTHOR'S PREFACE

The decade since 1930 has seen noteworthy shifts in Japan's foreign policy. These shifts have been accompanied by equally significant alterations in her internal economic, political and social structure. The purpose of this study is to discuss these internal developments.

After a brief description of the present structure and working of the Japanese Government, an attempt is made to explain the roles played in modern Japan by the various political, business, labor, rural and patriotic groups. As background for this, the main political events after September 1931 are outlined, showing the general trends within the country and the interrelations of the groups mentioned. It will be found that the most obvious characteristic of the new period is the added power and prestige gained by the services, especially by the Imperial Army. Since events at home and abroad have necessitated new policies both in centralization of control and regulation of the economic, social and financial life of the nation, these have also been analyzed. In addition, those aspects of Japanese life which are peculiar to Japan, and which are often the most difficult to interpret, have been considered as psychological factors, and have been supplemented by a short discussion of the influence of public opinion. The author concludes the study with a description of possible future trends and changes in Japanese politics and life.

A short explanation of the method of treatment is in order. The author is fully aware of the shortcomings of a survey of this sort, which had to be made without residence in Japan and without constant reference to all Japanese periodicals. Terms in many cases not entirely applicable to Japan like "fascist," "totalitarian," "democratic," have been used somewhat loosely for lack of a better nomenclature.

Certain subjects having perhaps as much bearing on Japan's development as any of those discussed, and already included in the *I. P. R. Inquiry Series* issued by the International Secretariat of the Institute of Pacific Relations, were purposely omitted. These include a study of the development of economic control in the early Meiji Period (1868-1912) to be found in E. H. Norman's *The Establishment of a Modern State in Japan* and America's role in the Pacific treated in T. A. Bisson's *American Far Eastern Policy 1931-1940*. Other studies, such as G. C. Allen's *Japanese Industry: Its Recent Development and Present Condition* and Miriam S. Farley's *The Problem of Japanese Trade Expansion in the Post-War Situation,* treat in detail subjects mentioned only briefly below. The work of Charles B. Fahs, *Government in Japan,* approaches the problem from a slightly different viewpoint and emphasizes trends and international parallels. Consequently, references in the footnotes to any of these documents usually indicate a more detailed presentation or a slightly different interpretation.

The problems treated are too complex to allow extreme simplification. To many the study may seem inconclusive and indeed it would be rash to forecast Japan's future development simply on the basis of a study of alterations in her internal structure. If, however, this outline has helped to clarify the complicated and ever-changing scene in Japan, it has then served its purpose.

CONTENTS

JAPAN SINCE 1931

CHAPTER I

THE STRUCTURE AND WORKING OF THE GOVERNMENT

It is the purpose of this chapter to discuss briefly the functions of the executive, legislative and judicial branches of the Japanese Government, especially as they have developed in recent years.[1] The vicissitudes of the framing and final promulgation of the Constitution are not important here[2] but it should always be remembered that the framers were less favorably inclined toward a democratic representative system than toward an oligarchical absolutism.[3] The first section of the five-article oath of the Emperor Meiji, issued in 1868, has assured the continuance of constitutional government even during a period of unchecked nationalism. This article states that "an assembly widely convoked shall be established, and thus great stress shall be laid upon public opinion."[4] The Constitution is rendered inflexible by the fact that the initiative for an amendment must come from the Throne and be approved by two-thirds of the attendance in the House. Thus far it has never been amended,[5] although its scope has been considerably broadened by the Imperial House Laws, which regulate the succession and administration of the Imperial family.

[1] For an excellent treatment of the subject as well as for translations of the various government documents at the time of the Restoration, see Harold S. Quigley, *Japanese Government and Politics*, New York, 1932; W. W. McLaren, "Japanese Government Documents," *Transactions of the Asiatic Society of Japan*, XLII, Part I, Tokyo, 1914; Robert K. Reischauer, *Japan-Government Politics*, Nelson and Son, New York, 1939, and Charles B. Fahs, "Government in Japan," I. P. R. Inquiry Series, International Secretariat Institute of Pacific Relations, New York, 1940.

[2] The commentaries of the Constitution of Hirobumi Ito, translated as: *Commentaries on the Constitution of the Empire of Japan*, 2d ed., Tokyo, 1906, are of great importance. Prince Ito is the leading authority on the interpretation of the Constitution inasmuch as he was president of the commission that drafted the Constitution. See also Kenneth Colegrove, "The Japanese Constitution," *The American Political Science Review*. Vol. XXXI, Dec. 1937, pp. 1027 *et seq.*

[3] Quigley, *op. cit.*, p. 42 *et seq.*

[4] McLaren, *op. cit.*, p. 8.

[5] Quigley, *op. cit.*, p. 46 *et seq.*

3

The Emperor

The Emperor is the head of the Japanese State in an absolutely unconditional sense. His position is described by Japanese writers as follows:

> The Imperial powers are in no sense circumscribed by the Constitution, of which (the) spirit is that the Emperor out of his benevolence and for the happiness of his subjects consults their will in the use of his powers, but not that the people of themselves possess any power.[6]

The fact that the ruler is the foundation of the State by virtue of his divine descent in unbroken succession from the grandson of the Sun Goddess, Amaterasu O Mikami, has not been challenged by the Constitution but rather strengthened by it.[7] The Emperor is the incarnate representative of the gods from whom he is descended and the fountainhead from which authority emanates. His subjects can exercise power only during his pleasure. A mere expression by the Emperor of regret or indignation can cause the resignation of a Government official, while anyone daring to express the belief that His Majesty is not inviolable receives the harshest punishment. The displeasure of the Emperor at the abortive *coup d'état* of February 26, 1936 is believed to account for the resignation of five out of the seven members of the Supreme War Council. Furthermore, upon formally opening the Imperial Diet on May 4, the Emperor acted contrary to precedent when he referred to the February 26 incident with regret.[8]

The executive functions of the Emperor include the making of appointments, receiving foreign envoys, signing treaties and ordinances, issuing rescripts, attendance at sessions of the Privy Council, conferences with his ministers and the declaration of war.[9] Actually the Emperor always acts in accordance with the recommendations of his advisers. However, he has

---

[6] Hidejiro Nagata, "Japanese Faith in the Imperial Household," *Hinode,* Oct. 1932. Quoted in *Contemporary Japan,* Dec. 1932, p. 524.

[7] Prince Ito writes: "The Sacred Throne of Japan is inherited from Imperial Ancestors, and is to be bequeathed to posterity; in it resides the power to reign over and govern the State. That express provisions concerning the sovereign power are specially mentioned in . . . the Constitution, in no wise implies that any newly settled opinion thereon is set forth. . . . On the contrary, the original national polity . . . is more strongly confirmed than ever." Ito, *Commentaries,* cited, 6. 2.

[8] *Oriental Economist,* Vol. III, No. 5, May 1936, p. 277.

[9] Kenneth Colegrove, "The Japanese Emperor," *The American Political Science Review,* Vol. XXVI, August and October, 1932, pp. 642-59 and 828-45.

much indirect influence in Japan because of the wealthy hold-ings of the Imperial family, a large civil list, and the social wel-fare sponsored by their Imperial Majesties. The Emperor is the symbol of national unity and his imponderable influence in Japan's modern political development has often made predic-tions of that development impossible.

The Cabinet

The Cabinet is the most important branch of the executive and acts as advisory agent to the Emperor. Although the Cab-inet is not specifically provided for in the Constitution, Article 55 stipulates that:

> The respective Ministers of State shall give their advice to the Emperor, and be responsible for it.
>
> All Laws, Imperial Ordinances and Imperial Rescripts, of whatever kind, that relate to the affairs of State require the countersignature of a Minister of State.[10]

On this basis a Cabinet has developed composed of the various Ministers of State, with the Prime Minister holding the senior position. During the period of their earliest development the Cabinets functioned smoothly under Princes Hirobumi Ito and Aritomo Yamagata, with the support of the various regional feudal influences, especially those of the Satsuma and Choshu clans.[11]

The first party Cabinet was that of Takashi Hara, formed in 1918, which contained party members for all the ministries except the services. There was no fixed policy in this regard, however, until 1924 when Count Takaaki Kato, President of the Kenseikai Party, formed a cabinet. Thereafter party cab-inets continued with varying degrees of success until the forma-tion of the Saito Ministry, a national government, following the political assassinations in May, 1932. From then until the forma-tion of the Planning Board in 1937, the Finance Ministry under Mr. Korekiyo Takahashi became the real center of interest and

---

[10] Translations of the Constitution can be found in Ito or Quigley.

[11] For excellent treatments of the Cabinet and its problems, see Kenneth Cole-grove, "The Japanese Cabinet," *The American Political Science Review*, Vol. XXX, No. 5, Oct. 1936, pp. 903-23, and "The Japanese Foreign Office," *American Journal of International Law*, Vol. 30, Oct. 1936, pp. 585 *et seq*. See also Yasushi Sekiguchi, "The Changing Status of the Cabinet in Japan," *Pacific Affairs*, Vol. XI, Mar. 1938, p. 6; and E. H. Norman, *The Establishment of a Modern State in Japan*, International Secretariat, Institute of Pacific Relations.

the usual executive functions of the Cabinet were diminished in a general trend toward centralization.[12]

The Privy Council

Another important executive branch of the government is the Privy Council. This organization of elderly statesmen, chosen for their distinctive careers, was established in 1888 and was until 1922 an especially important instrument in the hands of Prince Yamagata. Its primary function is "to serve as the highest body of the Emperor's constitutional advisers . . . with no leanings towards this or that party." All statutes, Imperial Ordinances and treaties must receive its approval. If it advises the Emperor contrary to the Cabinet, such advice is equivalent to Imperial disapproval of the views of the Cabinet. Such was the case when the Privy Council refused to approve an Imperial Ordinance granting relief to the Bank of Taiwan in April 1927, thus causing the downfall of the Wakatsuki Government.[13] In connection with the approval of treaties, it compelled the Government to repudiate the phrase, "in the name of their respective peoples" in the Pact of Paris, as this phrase was considered inconsistent with the provisions of the Japanese Constitution.[14] In spite of violent opposition from the services and the political jealousy of Count Myoji Ito as official spokesman for the opposing Seiyukai, the Council gave its approval to the London Naval Treaty in 1930. This approval may have been dictated to a large extent by pressure from public opinion, the press, the Lord Keeper of the Privy Seal and the Genro.

The Genro

The Genro was an institution peculiar to Japan. It was an advisory group entirely extra-constitutional, whose functions evolved from traditions rather than from any existing statute or ordinance. Its members included the leading spirits of the Restoration of 1868 and a number of those who held high government positions thereafter. Thus developed a group to advise the

[12] Shoji Iizawa, *Politics and Political Parties in Japan,* Tokyo, 1938, p. 29 *et seq.* The Okuma-Itagaki Cabinet of 1898 was not strictly a party cabinet.

[13] Kenneth Colegrove, "The Japanese Privy Council," *American Political Science Review,* Vol. XXV, Aug. and Nov. 1931, pp. 589-614 and 881-905 especially pp. 885 *et seq.* Ito, *op. cit.,* p. 99.

[14] H. S. Quigley, "The Privy Council vs. The Cabinet in Japan," *Foreign Affairs,* Vol. 9, April 1931, pp. 501 *et seq.* See also Fahs, *op. cit.,* p. 66 *et seq.*

Emperor in case of a deadlock between the Cabinet and the Council or any other government organs.[15] It became the group whose final judgment was never challenged, and whose role was particularly vital following the death of Emperor Meiji in 1912. In general, the *Genro* opposed democratic principles until after the death of Prince Yamagata in 1922, as all the members, with the exception of Prince Saionji, were clansmen, and a conservative attitude favored the continuation of clan influence. Since 1931 Prince Saionji, the sole surviving *Genro*, has been consistent in his opposition to fascist elements within Japan.

Until very recently Prince Saionji was always consulted first when a cabinet crisis arose, and his choice of premier invariably prevailed. In the late spring of 1932, following a series of political assassinations, he refused to countenance the demands of the army to make Baron Hiranuma the new premier and selected a moderate, Admiral Saito. Again, in 1934, Admiral Okada was chosen on the advice of the *Genro* in spite of opposition from the Privy Council. His liberalizing influence was obvious during the turbulent days at the end of February two years later.[16] Since Prince Saionji is now ninety-one years old, the question of the succession immediately suggests itself. However, it is now assumed that with him the institution of the *Genro* will pass away, and that possibly the special advisory power of this group will shift to the Lord Keeper of the Privy Seal, the President of the Privy Council and possibly others. In any case, so long as his present prestige and vitality last, Prince Saionji will be a dominating factor in determining the course which Japanese politics follow.

Another unique feature of Japanese Government is the unusually strong power of legislation by Imperial Ordinance. Professor Quigley maintains that it is greater than in any other constitutionally governed state, even pre-War Prussia. The administrative ordinance power deriving from Article 9 of the Constitution includes the right to declare war, to make peace and treaties, to prolong or prorogue the Diet, and to maintain peace and order through the police. It cannot alter any existing

---

[15] Quigley, *Japanese Government*, cited, p. 95 *et seq.*

[16] Causton, E. E. N., *Militarism and Foreign Policy in Japan*, London, 1936, p. 58 *et seq.* At the time of the formation of the Cabinet of Prince Konoye in June 1937 a new procedure was adopted. First the Emperor asked Lord Keeper of the Privy Seal Yuasa to confer with Baron Hiranuma, then President of the Privy Council. Next the *Genro* was consulted.

laws but only regulates measures for carrying out a particular law. Emergency ordinances are issued, under Article 8, when the Diet is not in session, to maintain public safety or to avert public calamities. Such ordinances must be approved by the Diet when it next meets, but in practice it has been virtually impossible to have them nullified. Finally, through emergency financial ordinances, which also require the approval of the Diet before they become law, the Government is equipped to meet further contingencies.[17]

Supreme Command

One of the most perplexing aspects of the Japanese system of Government is the exact function of the Supreme Command and the resulting "dual government." During the past few years the Occident has realized that the civil government may make some specific statement of policy and that the military authorities may immediately repudiate it by their action on the Asiatic mainland. This is the result of provisions in the Japanese Constitution and the interpretations that have been given them. Under Article 11 the Emperor is given supreme command of the army and navy while under Article 12 he "determines the organization and peace-standing of the Army and Navy." This is interpreted to mean that the control of the services is outside the purview of the usual State organs and outside the control of the Cabinet. Imperial Ordinances have laid it down that only a General or Lieutenant-General may serve as Minister of War and only an Admiral or a Vice-Admiral as Minister of the Navy. This greatly enhances the opportunity of the services to check the formation of a cabinet of which they do not approve. A signal example of this was the failure of General Ugaki to form a cabinet in January, 1937, when he was unable to secure a Minister of War of the proper rank willing to serve with him.[18]

The problem of dual government is further complicated by

[17] Ito, *op. cit.*, pp. 14, 17, and 134; Quigley, *op. cit.*, p. 119 *et seq.* In 1928 the Tanaka Ministry resorted to an Emergency Ordinance to make the Peace Preservation Law stricter when it knew the Diet would have opposed it when the new Diet met. In spite of general opposition it was impossible to rally enough support to revoke this ordinance. See Kenneth Colegrove, "The Japanese Emperor," *op. cit.*, p. 658.

[18] *Ibid.*, p. 830 *et seq.* For a concise account of the role of the military in Japan prior to 1936, see Kenneth W. Colegrove, *Militarism in Japan*, Boston, 1936, p. 18 *et seq.*

the fact that all officers of the high command have direct access to the Emperor as Commander-in-Chief of the army and navy. This includes the Minister of War and the Minister of the Navy who are responsible to the remainder of the cabinet in matters relating to the Supreme Command. Furthermore, the other advisory military organs such as the Boards of Marshals and Fleet Admirals, the General Staff and the Supreme War Council are independent of the cabinet and include no civilian representatives. In wartime the Supreme War Council is superseded by the Imperial Headquarters which is presided over by the Emperor. Thus, finding themselves independent of censure by the civil authorities, the services have often arbitrarily decided on their own course of action. The Foreign Office has then had the unpleasant task of explaining the situation as best it could. In conclusion it should be noted that, especially since July 1937, the difficulties resulting from "dual government" have been greatly reduced by all branches of the Government acting more in accord with the will of the military. There is still ample opportunity for the direction of policies by those behind the scenes.

The Diet

As already indicated, the legislative and judicial aspects of Japanese government are not so important as the executive. The main legislative organ, known as the Diet, is composed of a House of Peers (the Upper House) and a House of Representatives (the Lower House) convoked by the Emperor to deliberate upon new legislation. The House of Peers, made up of princes of the blood, princes and marquises, representatives of the other orders of the peerage and of the highest taxpayers, and Imperial appointees, numbered 409 members in 1937.[19] The 466 members of the House of Representatives have been elected by adult male suffrage since 1928. Deliberations are public except when a secret sitting is ordered by the Government or the Houses themselves. Bills may be introduced by the Government or by private members. In recent years, until the present war, the most important function of the Diet has

[19] For a more elaborate account of the Diet, its functions and powers, see Colegrove, "Powers and Functions of the Japanese Diet," *The American Political Science Review*, Vol. XXVII, December 1933, and Vol. XXVIII, February 1934; Quigley, *Japanese Government*, Chapters X and XI, p. 160 *et seq*; *The Japan Year Book 1938-39*, Tokyo, 1939, p. 109; Fahs, *op. cit.*, p. 71 *et seq*.

been the consideration of the budget. This is introduced to the Lower House first and its approval, though not legally binding, is assumed to carry with it the approval of the Peers. If the two houses fail to agree or if no budget is passed at all, that of the previous year automatically becomes effective. Other important functions of the Diet are the enactment of new taxes and the control of finances in general. The actions of the cabinet are checked though not actually controlled by interpellations from Diet members to the various cabinet ministers, requesting further details or explanations of their actions. A vote of non-confidence does not necessarily mean the resignation of the Government, although the Government attempts to avoid this embarrassment. The political parties and election returns were especially important during the period of party ascendancy when the cabinets were composed of members of the majority party in the House of Representatives. But in recent months they have been playing a progressively less important role.[20]

The Diet, as already indicated, has a check on the emergency ordinance power through its authority to disapprove ordinances issued during its recess, but in practice after an ordinance is once issued it is comparatively easy to obtain its acceptance. The Diet has no constitutional part in the conduct of foreign relations, but here again its influence is felt indirectly through interpellations and addresses of its members to the Throne. Thus the legislative arm is subordinate to the executive and, aside from its right to enact new legislation, its powers are distinctly limited.

The "Organic Theory" (Kikan Setsu)

Although the discussion between the two leading schools of jurists over the "Organic Theory" which raged relentlessly until the leader of the liberal group, Professor Tatsukichi Minobe, lost his seat in the Diet, seems purely academic on the surface, in reality it has had a profound influence on Japan's development. The discussion has centered around the interpretation of the phrase in Article 5 of the Constitution which states that "the Emperor exercises legislative power with the consent of the Imperial Diet." Professor Yatsuka Hozumi and his colleagues maintain that the Emperor is in no way an organ of the State but *is* the State. They explain that even though the

[20] See below p. 18.

Constitution recognizes the existence of various separate powers such as the executive and legislative, and of such organs of the State as the Imperial Diet, all the organs exercising these powers are subordinate to the Emperor. Professor Minobe, on the other hand, through a liberal interpretation of Article 5 maintains that the Diet is an independent organ and not an agent of the Emperor. It is, in fact, a representative organ reflecting the opinion of the people in giving consent to legislation.

It can be inferred from the above that if the interpretation given by Professor Minobe had been accepted, then the development of an authoritarian state would have been much less likely. Furthermore, he would have all ministers (including those of the services) responsible both individually and collectively to the Emperor for their own actions and that of the Cabinet to which they belong. This would mean that the Ministers of War and the Navy would be liable to effective censure both by the Emperor and the Cabinet, and it would forestall any independent action on the part of the military. It is not surprising, therefore, that the military and conservative elements in the Government rallied around Professor Hozumi and that pressure was put upon the liberal group until its interpretation was discarded. The way was then cleared, from the juridical viewpoint, for the creation of a centralized corporate state.[21]

The Judiciary

The judiciary was modeled chiefly on the French system and presents no unique aspects. The courts, divided into ordinary and administrative, fall within the Imperial prerogative, and the exercise of judicial power is entrusted to them in the name of the Emperor. Their personnel, selected by competitive examinations, is composed largely of men trained in the law schools of the Imperial universities, especially Tokyo.[22]

The structure of government, as it has developed in Japan, has not been without weaknesses. From the democratic viewpoint the most serious of these are: duality of government policy; the independence of the armed services; the fact that the ministers and cabinet are responsible to the Emperor and only indirectly to the electorate through the power of censure exercised by the members of the Lower House; the automatic re-

[21] Colegrove, "The Japanese Emperor," p. 648 *et seq.*
[22] Quigley, *op. cit.,* p. 273 *et seq.*

newal of the current budget if the Diet fails to pass a new one, and defects in the election system. The election law of 1925 permitted universal manhood suffrage for those over 25 and not on relief. This law has not been as effective as was hoped. Candidates have frequently spent five times the prescribed limit for campaign funds and the Government party always has an advantage since the Home Minister is in charge of elections and the Minister of Justice usually prosecutes only the law-breakers of the opposition.[23] The appointment in June 1938 of a Diet System Investigation Council indicates that there is some dissatisfaction with the present system. The changes which have been proposed include alterations in the membership of the House of Peers and the amendment of the electoral system in such a way as to aid minority candidates.[24] If Japan decides to continue the totalitarian type of government, the weaknesses mentioned above will be distinct assets to a strongly centralized ruling element.

[23] *Ibid.*, p. 252, *et seq.*

[24] *The Japan Times,* June 16, 1938. According to a statement in the *Asahi,* quoted in the *Japan Advertiser,* June 24, 1938, the results of the first meeting of the Council were not encouraging and the commissioners were not well posted on the proposed election reforms.

CHAPTER II

SOCIAL AND POLITICAL GROUPS

In a country like Japan, where freedom of individual action has always been limited, it is natural that the relationships of the various social and political groups should be of paramount importance. The individual expresses himself through the group to which he gives his allegiance, and the authorities have become sensitive to pressure not from individuals, but from coherent groups. Apart from his place in his family—which is broader in scope and responsibility than in the West—each individual is an integral part of some functional group.

In feudal days men were stereotyped as warriors, peasants, artisans, townsmen or merchants, and were prevented by law from changing classes. But more recently the significant categories have been the small landowners and peasants, small manufacturers and shop-keepers, industrial and merchant groups, and finally the governing groups, comprising the bureaucracy, the services and the intelligentsia.[1] Although the struggle for power has led to varying degrees of amalgamation between different elements, the following groups may be distinguished for the purposes of the present discussion: the financiers and industrialists; the politicians and political parties; the rural and labor groups; and finally the militarists and the patriotic societies.

Financial and Industrial Groups

In considering the role played in contemporary Japan by the financial and industrial groups, it must be remembered that the shift from an agricultural to an industrial economy is still incomplete and that agriculture and small trading continue to engage the bulk of Japanese labor. The purchasing power of

[1] Kunio Yamagata, "Japan's Social Solidarity," *Contemporary Japan,* Dec. 1934, p. 388 *et seq.* The above classification is taken from G. C. Allen, *Japan the Hungry Guest,* London, 1938, p. 65. These categories are large but not all-inclusive as they fail to provide for agricultural laborers, tenants and factory workers as such.

the masses has thus remained small and industrialization has necessitated an expansion of foreign markets and the simultaneous creation of a strong army and navy to secure a share in the markets on the Asiatic continent. Industrialization also required a supply of capital. At first there was a lack of accumulated mercantile capital, and the Government refused to borrow abroad because of the risk of foreign penetration. However, it willingly secured funds by taxation and lent them to industry. Thus there developed a system of subsidies and a close partnership between industrial and Government groups.[2]

The World War boom in the arms industry created a new and small plutocracy. The Tokyo earthquake of 1923 and the financial panic of 1927 further accelerated the concentration of financial control and left the three leading companies, Mitsui, Mitsubishi and Sumitomo, holding one-fourth of the nation's private capital and the "Big Eight" controlling 37.6 per cent of the bank deposits, 72.9 per cent of the trust properties and 25.9 per cent of the liability reserves of insurance companies.[3]

These financial groups felt that their wealth warranted more political power than they had through their representation in the House of Peers. The Mitsui interests tried to obtain more power by supporting the Seiyukai Party, a political group. Their attempt was frustrated not only by the new franchise and corruption in the political parties but also by the formation of a national Government in 1932. Thereafter, hoping to secure both influence and profits for themselves, they shifted their allegiance to the generals when the military and naval appropriations were increased by half a million yen in March, 1936. The recent rise to power of Mr. Ikeda, the manager since 1933 of the Mitsui interests, is typical of the efforts made by the leading industrialists to keep on good terms with the military leaders.[4] Mr. Ikeda was made a governor of the Bank of Japan so that he would be in a position to change the regulations of

[2] Saburo Matsukata, "A Historical Study of Japanese Capitalism," *Pacific Affairs*, VII, p. 71 *et seq.*, and William Holland and Kate Mitchell, editors, *Problems of the Pacific, 1936*, London, 1937, p. 84 *et seq.*

[3] Joseph Barnes and Frederick V. Field, *Behind the Far Eastern Conflict*, Institute of Pacific Relations, New York, 1933, p. 13.

[4] For a description of some of the key men in the largest financial and industrial concerns, see *Fortune*, Sept. 1936. Mr. Ikeda was born in 1867, and is a Harvard graduate; he joined the Mitsui Bank in 1895 and became managing director of the Mitsui interests until 1936. *Japan-Manchoukuo Year Book*, 1938, p. 989.

the bank in order to allow the diversion of adequate funds for the expansion of heavy industry. Later he became Finance Minister.[5] A similar situation confronted the Mitsubishi companies of the Iwasaki family. The Mitsubishi gave its support to the leading rival political party, the Minseito, and consequently was in favor of Baron Shidehara's conciliatory policy toward China prior to September, 1931. But it was quick to take advantage of the profits to be derived from a semi-wartime economy in Manchuria. The third great company, the Sumitomo, had close connections with influential government officials, for the present head of the family, Baron Kichizaemon Sumitomo, is the nephew of Prince Saionji, the *Genro*. Under the able directorship of Masatsune Ogura the Sumitomo interests pressed for the development of alloys and aluminum and were in an excellent position to profit from the munitions boom.[6]

As long as heavy industry remained undeveloped and the Government pursued a liberal policy allowing free access to the supplies of raw cotton, the textile industries prospered, centering especially around Osaka. Recent restrictions have greatly hampered their activities. The Government's policies have been supported, however, by the old financial houses, as well as by new interests like those of Mr. Aikawa of the Manchurian Industrial Development Corporation and Mr. Fusanosuke Kuhara who received a monopoly to supply the government's steel plants of Yawata with ore.

The National Mobilization Law of 1937 has ruled out independent action on the part of the industrialists. Although the banking houses are absorbing their share of the new Government loans, it can be predicted with a degree of certainty that unless these interests receive a fair return on their investments in the new industries, they will again shift their allegiance from the military to some other group. Even if they are assured a certain minimum return by the new legislation, it is conceivable that continued government spending and an

[5] The development of the Mitsui interests from a feudal banking institution to a modern syndicate is treated in *The House of Mitsui, A Record of Three Centuries,* Tokyo, 1933, and Oland D. Russell, *The House of Mitsui,* Boston, 1939. For an account of the four leading concerns, the *Zaibatsu,* see G. C. Allen, "The Concentration of Economic Control in Japan," *Economic Journal,* June 1937.

[6] *Fortune,* September 1936, p. 168 *et seq.*

unfavorable balance of trade may persuade these interests to champion a new cause rather than see their holdings diminish through inflation. If, however, they are forced to choose between continuance of the capitalistic State rigidly controlled by the Government and a new social order, they will undoubtedly choose the former.

The Political Parties

The development of political parties in Japan since the emergence of constitutional government in 1889 has been complicated and for many years they were unable to exert any real influence. The Constitutional Reform Party (Rikken Kaishuto), under the leadership of Shigenobu Okuma, believed that the happiness of the exclusive few could not coexist with the dignity and prosperity of the Imperial Household and the well-being of the people at large. This party was a predecessor of the Minseito. Another early party, formed by Taisuke Itagaki, was the Liberal Party (Jiyuto). It was inspired by an equally high ideal. Itagaki said that "it behooves us to organize a Liberal Party and to develop a spirit of cooperation among ourselves, so that we may develop our heaven-born liberty against the oppression of artificial power and cultivate a spirit of self-government."[7] From this developed the rival party, the Seiyukai.

The parties had to pass through a long period of compromise before they were sufficiently developed to form a two-party rivalry. Even in 1918, when the Hara Ministry selected a cabinet largely from the Seiyukai, the three important portfolios of Foreign Affairs, War and Navy were not held by members of this party. It was not until 1924 that the parties reached maturity. In this year, Mr. Takaaki Kato, President of the Kenseikai (a forerunner of the Minseito), formed a government which succeeded in introducing the bill for manhood suffrage in the following year. For eight years thereafter, the normal Western parliamentary procedure was followed, power shifting from one party to another.

[7] Shoji Iizawa, *op. cit.*, p. 12 *et seq.* This pamphlet by an editorial writer of one of Japan's industrial newspapers is a concise account of parties in Japan. For a study of parties which were first organized in 1880, see: A. H. Lay, "A Brief Sketch of the History of Political Parties in Japan," *Transactions Asiatic Society of Japan*, Vol. XXX, 1903, p. 363 *et seq.*, and Shigenobu Okuma, *Fifty Years of New Japan*, London, 1910, Vol. I, Chapter IV.

In 1927, during a period of financial crisis, the Seiyukai Party was victorious under the leadership of Baron Giichi Tanaka, despite the shadow on his reputation owing to an alleged misappropriation of funds while he was War Minister in a previous cabinet. This was the beginning of a period of accusations and recriminations by both parties, which exposed their corruption and spelled their defeat a few years later. The Tanaka Ministry lost much prestige through the resignation of Finance Minister Korekiyo Takahashi, the interference of its Home Minister, Kisaburo Suzuki, in the first general elections of February 1928, and the promulgation of reactionary measures to suppress radicals. When the implications of the death of General Chang Tso-lin, the former Manchurian warlord, became too embarrassing, the Ministry resigned and Yuko Hamaguchi, President of the Minseito, was asked to form a government. At best the parties were making a poor start.

The Minseito Government took office in 1929 when Japan was entering a period of depression. To overcome this disadvantage, the party platform included promises of a return to the gold standard, retrenchment and deflation, but such measures only aggravated the existing difficulties. In the field of foreign relations, the friendly attitude of Foreign Minister Shidehara toward China provided a sounder basis for trade expansion than had the previous policies, but it was anathema to the militarists, as were the increasing popularity of disarmament and the reduction of defense expenditures. The ratification of the London Naval Treaty on April 22, 1930, had also been a blow to the prestige of the Navy. Little wonder, therefore, that the Minseito Party was completely demoralized by the attempted assassination of its leader in November 1930. His resignation shortly afterward was the signal for the selfish cliques within the party to assert themselves in such a way as to weaken irretrievably the cause of party government. Mr. Kenzo Adachi, the Home Minister, was eager to become the new party president; while Mr. Inouye, the Finance Minister, and his group had Baron Shidehara appointed *interim* premier. Even the appointment of Mr. (now Baron) Wakatsuki, a former premier, could not stem the tide of opposition. A coalition movement launched by the Home Minister, the growing demand for a strong policy toward China and the dissatisfaction with the whole policy of retrenchment were factors sufficient to return the Seiyukai to power under the premiership of Mr. Inukai.[8]

The Seiyukai won a sweeping victory at the polls by taking advantage of a changing attitude at home, promising relief through firm diplomacy toward China, and profiting directly from the assassination of ex-Finance Minister Inouye in early February 1932 (which incidentally deprived the Minseito of its campaign manager and some sorely needed funds). Little real interest was shown by the people at large in the elections, for they were slowly realizing that the military were beginning to direct Japan's foreign policy. This was a natural result of the military's superior knowledge of Manchuria and of their having already worked out plans for its development, while liberals who took an interest in politics were entirely absorbed by the less important task of internal social reform.[9] Following their victory in February, the Seiyukai developed a "Five-Year Plan" in which its author, Mr. Jotaro Yamamoto, pleaded for government control of industries and electric power, a decrease in freight rates, lower interest rates and encouragement of productive enterprises, stimulation of manufacturing industries, control of imports, revision of tariff schedules and finally the formulation of new industrial policies for Korea and Formosa.[10] But reform proposals had come too late to be carried out by either of the leading parties. The murder of the new Seiyukai Premier, Mr. Tsuyoshi Inukai, on May 15, 1932, made the people feel more keenly the pressure of the emergency period.

The increasingly important role played by the army in the formation of the new cabinet and the policies adopted immediately after May 1932 and again after February 1936 will be treated later. Here it should be noted that the parties were inadequately prepared to play a leading role. Not only was the Minseito politically impotent following the elections, but it had not yet recovered from the deaths of Hamaguchi and Inouye. In anticipation of a summons to form a new govern-

[8] A more detailed account of the political events during this period will be found in Masamichi Royama, "Politics at Home," *Contemporary Japan*, Vol. I, No. 1, June 1932, p. 74 *et seq*. See below p. 39. An interesting study might be made of the question whether the change in the anti-foreign movement in China from an anti-British to an anti-Japanese one was the cause or result of the new strong Japanese policy toward China.

[9] Shigeharu Matsumoto, "Party Battles in Japan," *Pacific Affairs*, April 1932, p. 302 *et seq*.

[10] Royama, *op. cit.*, p. 79. See also Fahs, *op. cit.*, p. 77.

ment, the Seiyukai nominated the Home Minister, Dr. Kisaburo Suzuki, as president. But the parties had overplayed their hands and were passed over by Prince Saionji, while Baron Hiranuma, the choice of the army, also was ignored. Both elements were placated, however, by a compromise in the allocation of cabinet posts; the army was satisfied to have Count Uchida, the former president of the South Manchurian Railway, as Foreign Minister and General Araki as War Minister, while domestic affairs were placed under the control of three Seiyukai and two Minseito ministers.[11] In spite of the fact that the Seiyukai held nearly three-fourths of the seats in the Lower House, the absence of a controlling force within the party made it politically powerless. Finally in 1934, when Admiral Okada was asked to form a government, the parties refused to give it their support and three members of the Seiyukai Party were given posts within the cabinet only after they had severed their political connections.[12] Thus ended ignominiously the short role which parties have played in Japanese politics, for during the formation of new governments in 1936 and 1937 they were practically ignored. Much interest attached to the elections of February 1936, for the issue was whether the nationalist Government led by Admiral Okada would continue with Minseito help. The returns confirmed the Minseito's primacy in the Diet and gave it a majority when amalgamated with the new *Showakai*. Premier Okada and his cabinet seemed assured of an easy future until the coup of February 1936 drew attention to the need for a powerful national cabinet. Since that time the position of the parties has become even less significant.[13] For instance, following the resignation of Dr. Suzuki, differences within the Seiyukai Party resulted in its failure to elect a new president until May 1939 when Mr. Fusanosuke Kuhara finally assumed that office. A newspaper statement that the conflict within the Seiyukai over the question of a new president reflects the evils of the political parties,[14] is typical of the public attitude concerning them; their lack of leadership when the National Mobilization Bill was struggling through the Diet is indicative of how they have been neglected

[11] Iizawa, *op. cit.*, p. 38 *et seq.*
[12] *Ibid.*, p. 40.
[13] *Ibid.*, p. 41.
[14] *Asahi*, June 2, 1938, printed in the *Japan Advertiser*, June 4, 1938.

even by their own leaders.[15] Apart from the corruption and self-interest displayed by the parties throughout the short decade in which they occupied a prominent position, their impotency may have been due also to the imperfect operation of the parliamentary form of government and to "the immature stage at which the Japanese people as a whole find themselves in their progress toward political education."[16] Certainly national mobilization for the purpose of waging a successful war gives little opportunity to further this "political education." The prospects of a reassumption of leadership by the old political parties in the immediate future are slight.

Rural Organizations

In feudal Japan the farmer was the economic foundation of the State and today Japan is still largely an agrarian country. Although it is becoming self-sufficient in foodstuffs, the general situation of the farmers leaves much to be desired. Had the leaders of Japan's economic development thrown the nation's energies into agriculture immediately following the Restoration in 1868, Japan would have been able to supply practically all the needs of a simple agrarian people. However, military necessity and the menace of foreign powers encouraged a policy of industrialization and a consequent neglect of agricultural interests.[17] The result is that while 48.4 per cent of the gainfully employed were engaged in agriculture in 1930,[18] the majority of the population owned a very small portion of the aggregate wealth; for instance, those owning less than $500 worth of property or with an income of less than $400 comprised 84.6 per cent of the population and contributed 57 per

[15] *Tokyo Asahi Shimbun,* June 3, 1938.

[16] Matsumoto, *op. cit.,* p. 305. In spite of a resolution adopted in December 1939 by 240 members of parliament from various political parties, inviting the Cabinet to consider proper steps regarding resignation, it is doubtful whether the parties as such will play a decisive role in any new Cabinet in the near future. Even this resolution, approved by over half the members of the Lower House, did not threaten disapproval of the budget or a vote of nonconfidence at the next session of parliament. See *New York Times,* Dec. 27, 1939.

[17] Barnes and Field, *Behind the Far Eastern Conflict,* cited, p. 8. For Japan's early industrialization, see E. H. Norman, *op. cit.*

[18] Frederick V. Field, ed. *Economic Handbook of the Pacific Area,* New York, 1934, p. 10. *The Japan Year Book, 1938-9* estimates 44.9 per cent in agriculture and 2.3 per cent in fisheries.

cent of the national revenue in excises and indirect taxes. In 1933, the national debt was estimated to average $400 (about ¥1500 at that time) per farming family.[19]

Despite the general distress, the farming class has contributed generously to Japan's development. Their contribution began in the Meiji Period (1868-1912) when the farmers filled the state coffers with funds and the regiments of the army with their sons, on a sufficient scale to make possible successful wars against both China and Russia. Subsequently they continued to pay heavy taxes while certain industries received State subsidies. Industry also demanded cheap labor, and the farms not only provided a limitless supply but were compelled during the depression to absorb the unemployed as they returned to their homes. Not only had the silk market declined, but the middle-class urban dwellers were reducing their rice consumption, and these factors aggravated the agricultural situation.[20] The renewed demand for cheap male labor in the growing munitions industries and for female workers in the flourishing textile plants came as a welcome relief in the early thirties, and it was comparatively easy for the farmer to regard the adventures of the military with favor. However, the ever-increasing campaigns since 1937 have drawn heavily on the farms for manpower and have increased their financial hardships. Investigations in the fall of 1937 revealed that few men were working the farms.[21]

Because of these unfavorable economic circumstances, the small-scale farmer, according to some, "will be obliged sooner or later to prepare for a desperate campaign against the existing economic system."[22] In fact some doubt has arisen as to whether the agrarian group will continue to champion the cause of the military as enthusiastically as it has in the past. The *coup d'état* attempted in the middle of May 1932 by a rural organization,

[19] Barnes and Field, *Behind the Far Eastern Conflict*, p. 15. For the economic position of agriculture and government policies undertaken to alleviate the situation, see below p. 91 *et seq*. The debt is usually given as about ¥1000.

[20] Akira Kazami, "Whither the Japanese Peasantry?" *Contemporary Japan*, Vol. II, No. 4, p. 685.

[21] Galen M. Fisher, "The Cooperative Movement In Japan," *Pacific Affairs*, Vol. XI, No. 4, December 1938, p. 490.

[22] Kazami, *op. cit.*, p. 684. Mr. Kazami was a member of Parliament at the time, representing the group called Kokumin Domei, the vociferous party organized by Mr. Adachi, the Home Minister in the Minseito Ministry of Hamaguchi, and Wakatsuki, the Chief Secretary in the Konoye Cabinet.

the *Aikyo Juku*, and a reactionary society, the Blood Brotherhood League, showed the potential power of the rural groups if properly organized. Although this coup was unsuccessful, the group of zealous farmers and young naval officers involved in it, believing ardently that self-government based on agriculture was essential and that political parties and financial interests were responsible for the predicament of the country, did succeed in killing Premier Inukai and in attacking the Bank of Japan, the headquarters of the parties, the police and power stations.[23] Despite this coup, any widespread rural unrest seems unlikely, for the majority of the peasantry is conservative and loyal to the Throne, and the present Government-sponsored cooperative movement tends to dissolve any dangerously subversive elements.

This cooperative movement, which now boasts a membership of over six million, is the most powerful rural organization in Japan. It is described by its advocates as the stronghold of the nation in the days of depression and a democratic experiment in economics.[24] The cooperative movement in Japan was founded by Viscount Shinagawa, Home Minister in 1891, and Count T. Hirata, Director of the Legislation Bureau, both of whom had been greatly influenced by the German system. There had already been in existence in the feudal period mutual financing societies known as *Ko*, and credit guilds, first established in 1843 by Sontoku Ninomiya. In spite of the fact that a bill submitted to the Diet in 1891 authorizing the establishment of credit societies was killed because of a dissolution of the Diet, the Hypothec Bank and local agricultural and industrial banks were established in 1896. Their object was to supply to farmers and industrialists cheap capital secured on their immovable property. In 1900 a preliminary bill for credit, purchase, sales and production cooperatives was passed, and five years later Count Hirata organized the Central Union of Cooperative

[23] "Y," "The May 15 Case," *Contemporary Japan*, Sept. 1933, Vol. II, No. 2, p. 195 *et seq.*

[24] Compare two articles by Tadao Wikawa, "Our Cooperative Movement," *Contemporary Japan*, Vol. I, No. 3, 1932, p. 431 *et seq.*, and "Recent Strides in Our Cooperative Movement," *Contemporary Japan*, Vol. VI, 1937, p. 28. Mr. Wikawa, a member of the Finance Ministry and of former financial commissions to both China and Russia, is now comptroller of the Central Bank of Cooperative Societies. The more recent article by Galen M. Fisher, brings the subject down to date. See footnote 21.

Societies in Japan with 1,671 societies and a membership of 68,730.[25]

The cooperative movement grew rapidly. In 1911 it was aided by a gift of ¥20,000 from the Emperor Meiji; in 1917 it was recognized by the Urban Credit Societies; shortly afterwards, warehouses were planned for farming villages largely under the auspices of the cooperatives; in 1925 the National Federation of Purchase Societies, the cooperative bank with ¥30,000,-000 capital, was formed, and in the following year the Central Union entered the International Cooperative League. The movement was further encouraged by the support of Mr. Toyohiko Kagawa, head of cooperative stores in Osaka and Kobe and one of the leaders of the labor movement. The most important business of the cooperatives was the granting of credits. Of the 15,400 societies in 1937, all but 2,000 were loan associations located in agricultural villages. The following table will clarify the development of the movement.[26]

Year	Number of Societies	Membership
1903		68,730
1905	1,671	
1910	7,308	
1913	10,455	
1918	12,523	1,878,450
1922	14,047	2,734,695
1925	14,517	
1931	14,163	
1932	14,352	4,978,248
1936	15,460	6,147,922

The 28th Cooperative Congress, encouraged by the growth of the movement but realizing the necessity for further expansion and for more emphasis on trading and purchasing, adopted a new five-year plan at its meeting in 1932. This plan, to be inaugurated at the beginning of 1933, contemplated a 15 per cent increase in the number of societies and an increase of 59 per cent in membership. Such an expansion would have brought into the cooperatives approximately 60 per cent of the households in Japan. Unfortunately neither of these goals was attained. However, other aspects of the plan were also important. As recent deposits in the cooperative banks had declined to slightly over a billion yen, it was hoped to double this amount.

[25] Fisher, *op. cit.*, p. 480.

[26] *Ibid.*, p. 480 *et seq.*, and Wikawa, "Recent Strides in Our Cooperative Movement," p. 29, *et seq.*

By the end of 1936 they had increased by slightly over 50 per cent, or by ¥504,210,000, with only one year remaining to reach the goal. Similarly, the Central Union hoped to increase its membership of the cooperatives from 81 to 100 per cent and the membership of the Central Bank from 79 to 100 per cent. Another aspect of the plan was an attempt to fund the cooperator's debts and liquidate the frozen loans of the societies. The Deposit Bureau of the Finance Ministry advanced ¥100,000,000 and the Diet authorized the Central Bank to be reimbursed up to ¥30,000,000 for losses sustained in the liquidation.[27]

An encouraging sign of the growth of the movement since 1933 is the increased circulation of the monthly journal, *Ie no Hikari* (Light of the Home), from $1/4$ million to $1\frac{1}{4}$ million. It is claimed that the profits derived from this magazine defray the expenses of the movement, the cost of constructing the Cathedral of Cooperation in Tokyo for the Union and the latter's magazines, school and club.[28]

One of the most important features of the whole cooperative movement is the Central Chest (or Bank) for the Cooperative Societies (*Sangyo Kumiai Chuo Kinko*), established in 1923. So important has it become in recent years that, with its various branches, it has recently been admitted as a supporting member of the Bank of Japan. The following table shows its development:

	End of 1932	1936
Number of Federated Unions and Societies	11,472	11,945
Capital Subscribed	30,700,000 (in yen)	30,700,000 (in yen)
Capital Paid-up	30,318,560	30,700,000
Reserves	2,631,846	4,144,701
Borrowings	13,824,557	22,653,890
Cooperative Bonds Issued (subscribed by the Treasury Bureau)	59,503,000	82,837,980
Deposits Received	80,003,664	103,543,887
Loans	130,373,180	164,121,873
National Loan Bonds	18,493,269	64,648,630

The bank showed an increase in all its functions, although one not commensurate with the growth in membership in the societies over the corresponding period. The notable increase in

[27] Wikawa, "Our Cooperative Movement," p. 435. In connection with the total deposits in the banks estimated at $1\frac{1}{2}$ billion yen, it should be noted their loans amount to approximately 1 billion yen. *Japan Year Book, 1938-9*, p. 459.

[28] Wikawa, "Recent Strides in Our Cooperative Movement," p. 28.

National Loan Bonds absorbed is indicative of policies followed by all Japanese banks, and the bonds subscribed to by the Treasury Deposit Bureau show the close connection of the Bank with the central financial organs.[29]

The Japanese cooperative movement is not closely associated with the labor movement as in other countries, largely because of the Government's repression of labor. On the other hand, the close association of the movement with the Government has resulted in nearly half of the societies being "guaranteed as to financial responsibility" under Government pressure. Under this plan all capital and an agreed amount per member must be applied to meet financial obligations.[30] Such action is an attempt to reduce the high mortality rate of new societies prevalent since 1927. The cooperatives have helped in the control of seasonal price fluctuations by their planning and crop storage. Their power of independent action has been limited by their close association with both national and provincial officials, while in the elections of 1935 both the Central Union and the Young Men's Cooperative Alliance decided to support any candidate, regardless of his political affiliations, if he would sponsor the cooperative movement.

Herein lies perhaps one of the most important features not only of the cooperative movement but of all the agrarian groups. Their six million membership constitutes an excellent nucleus around which any farm program, political or economic, might be centered. The army is reported still in sympathy with the movement so that its continuance is thus assured. Under parts of the General Mobilization Law, the cooperatives may be used as agents in mobilizing national resources and thus may be a deciding factor in solving the problem of farm labor and food shortage. The recent announcement that $1\frac{1}{2}$ million fishermen would join the Union, the extension of cheap credit and fertilizer supply and the purchase of machinery by the Govern-

[29] *Ibid.*, p. 33. Figures given elsewhere give a less encouraging picture; for instance, it is noted that of the ¥30,700,000 paid up capital mentioned above, ¥15,000,000 has been subscribed by the Government. Other figures differ as follows:

	1936	1937
Cooperative debentures	¥ 86,575,000	¥ 82,939,000
Fixed deposits	99,383,000	80,776,000
Loans	147,419,000	155,565,000

[30] Fisher, *op. cit.*, p. 483.

ment and its operation through the cooperatives may have profound effects on Japanese agriculture.[31]

Through the cooperatives approximately half of the households in Japan can be reached immediately, and thus assistance can be rendered or, in case of emergency, the cooperatives can be used to make further demands on the peasants. If excessively drastic demands were made, these organizations might become uncontrollable and the peasants might resort to uprisings, even on pain of death, as they did in feudal Japan.[32] It seems more likely however that these societies, because of their close affiliations with the Government, will serve admirably as agents of the central authorities for the quick destruction of subversive elements. Through National Public Health Insurance, the organization of labor squads to assist families lacking manpower, and the increasing leniency of the Government in extending credits and adjusting debts, the discomforts of the agrarian communities may be alleviated and the danger of a lower production of foodstuffs may be avoided. Thus the six million cooperative members may become a tremendous asset to the State in its present program.

Labor and Radical Groups

An understanding of the Japanese labor movement is difficult because of the constant shifts and changes in the attitudes of the various groups.[33] Formed in 1912 the Laborer's Friendly Society (*Yuaikai*) was long the chief labor organization; it was founded by Bunji Suzuki and patterned in general on the American Federation of Labor. This Society contained seventy-one trade union organizations with a membership of 30,000.[34] The growth of this comparatively conservative group was greatly

[31] *Ibid.*, p. 490.

[32] Between 1603 and 1867, a period when communications were exceedingly crude, when there was no integrated movement among the peasantry and uprisings were forbidden, 1,153 peasant uprisings, largely directed against unbearable economic conditions, were recorded. An inarticulate peasantry, together with discontented tenants, might resort to this sort of action today, but will be likely to do so only if the present war brings more severe hardships than those existing at the moment. See Hugh Borton, "Peasant Uprisings in Japan of the Tokugawa Period," *Transactions Asiatic Society of Japan*, 2nd series, Vol. XVI, May 1938, p. 39.

[33] Recent policies leading to the amelioration or reform of either the agrarian problems or those of the industrial population are discussed below, p. 87 *et seq.*

[34] T. Baba, "Trade Unions and the Labour Movement," *Contemporary Japan*, Vol. I, No. 1, June 1932, p. 89 *et seq.*

hampered by the bellicose attitude assumed by the radical parties and labor groups immediately following the World War. From 1919 to 1923 Marxism became popular among professors and liberal intellectual leaders, radical writings were translated, and with the success of the Soviets before them, the leaders advocated the immediate establishment of a Communist State.[35] The first May Day parade was held in 1920 and two years later the first Communist Party was formed. The following year nearly two hundred persons were arrested during the May Day demonstrations and their leader was killed.[36] This same period also witnessed strikes in the Ashio Copper Mines, the Yawata Iron Foundry and the Kobe steel works.

The passage of the Universal Suffrage Act in 1925 inspired labor to form political parties and to attempt reforms through legislation. As a second Communist Party had just been formed, the Government considered that it had sufficient excuse for the passage of a Peace Preservation Law, and subsequently subversive acts of the Party and an increase in its membership to 27,500 led to further repressive measures in the form of an amendment of this law by emergency ordinance in 1928. The arrests which followed this action bore witness to its effectiveness as well as to the widespread fear of "red terrorism."[37] Meanwhile the various interpretations given to the role which labor should play in politics led to innumerable dissensions within the movement.

The earliest attempts at the formation of a unified party, largely sponsored by the Japanese Farmers' Union (*Nippon Nomin Kumiai*), brought these differences of opinion to a head in 1925. The new party, the Farmer Labor Party (*Nomin Rodoto*), received its support from the center group of the unions. It was opposed to direct action and advocated such reforms as the "reduction in armaments, tenant rights, social insurance, the legalization of strikes, and the collective bargain."[38] This party, accused of having a secret Communist platform, was

[35] Harada, *Labor Movement*, p. 189.

[36] This was Sakao Osugi, leader of the syndicalist element. See John Paul Reed, *Kokutai, A Study of Japanese Nationalism*, unpublished MS, University of Chicago, 1937, p. 79.

[37] For a summary of the communist movement see Quigley, *op. cit.*, p. 246, *et seq.*; and "A.," "The Rise and Fall of Japanese Communism," *Contemporary Japan*, Vol. II, No. 3, December 1933, p. 444 *et seq.*

[38] Kenneth Colegrove, "Labor Parties in Japan," *The American Political Science Review*, Vol. XXIII, No. 2, May 1929, p. 344.

dissolved by the Home Minister almost immediately after its inception. Following this, a second group, the Labor Farmer Party (*Rodo Nominto*), composed of right and center labor factions, was organized in March 1926. Its platform was so moderate that it was allowed to continue as an organization, but dissension within its ranks soon made it almost impotent politically. The third group, led by Bunji Suzuki, joined Professor Abe and his group of intellectuals. It was known as the Social Democratic Party (*Shakai Minshuto*) and adopted a platform similar to that of the Labor Farmer Party. Its program included extension of the franchise, lengthening of the parliamentary sessions, depriving the Upper House of its right to correct a budget adopted by the Lower House, a program of labor and social legislation and a farm tenancy law. Subsequently a fourth group, the Japanese Labor Farmer Party (*Nippon Ronoto*), was formed by Mr. Hisashi Aso and the Miner's Union as a challenge to the leadership of Mr. Suzuki.[39]

In the 1928 election, four proletarian parties won eight seats in the Lower House. The Social Democratic Party extended its platform to include demands for the reduction of rents, tenancy stipends and interest on loans, the guarantee of the right to till the soil for the farmers who worked it, and the legalization of birth control. They opposed the rationalization of industry. Before the election of 1930, a new party, the Proletarian Mass Party (*Musan Taishuto*), was formed. This new party asked for a guarantee of the right of the masses to live, the enactment of a law for capital punishment of corrupt officials, the abolition of bad taxes, and relief for the unemployed. Finally a new Labor Farm Party, centering its fight upon a reduction in the demands made upon the farmers and its opposition to imperialistic wars, elected one of its members to parliament.[40]

Because much had been lost by internal dissension, and as a partial reflection of the unifying effect of a growing nationalism after 1931, there developed a trend toward amalgamation. The Communist Party and radical elements had been effectively eliminated by arrests. The Proletarian Mass Party allied itself

[39] *Ibid.*, p. 346. Of these four groups, the Social Democratic Party in 1928 claimed a membership of 200,000, which, they maintained, was two-thirds of the organized workers and gave them the right to represent labor. See Mitsu Kohno, *Labour Movement in Japan*, Tokyo, 1938, p. 18 *et seq.*

[40] Quigley, *op. cit.*, p. 238 *et seq.*

with various small groups and in July 1932 formed, with its affiliates and the Social Democratic Party, the Social Mass Party (*Shakai Taishuto*) under the presidency of Professor Abe. Until recently the latter has been the only effective representative of 350,000 to 400,000 organized workers out of a total of 4½ million. That this party never seriously challenged Japan's program of continental expansion is evident from their statements regarding the Manchurian question. Though divided in sentiment, the party issued a declaration in favor of protecting Japan's rights and interests in Manchuria after 1931. Its program of foreign policy was outlined as follows:

Japan, having a special peasant structure inherent in all Asiatic countries, must endeavor to organize an Eastern policy, aiming at the unification of all opposition forces in Asia which demand independence and self-determination, "people's revolutions," "people's independence" and "resistance of the peasantry to imperialism."[41]

The former secretary of the Social Mass Party, Mr. Katsumaro Akamatsu, formed the fascist Japan State Socialist Party (*Nippon Kokka Shakaito*), which advocated the abolition of Parliament and capitalism and the granting of absolute power to the Emperor.[42]

The ensuing years witnessed continued unification under the leadership of the Social Mass Party. It advocated international cooperation and a world economic congress as the only rational way to combat fascism, and its domestic policy aimed at the reduction of the financial burdens of the masses and the stabilization of their national livelihood through State control of important industries and proper labor legislation. The party was opposed equally to fascism and communism.[43] In the elections of February 1936 it won 18 seats in the Lower House, six times its previous representation; and when General Hayashi dissolved Parliament in the spring of 1937 and the Social Mass Party opposed him as a fascist, it increased its representation to 37.[44]

[41] *Tokyo Nichi-Nichi*, October 2, 1932, quoted in O. Tanin and E. Yohan, *Militarism and Fascism in Japan*, New York, 1934, p. 246.

[42] *Ibid.*, p. 237. The temporary amalgamation early in 1939 of the Social Mass Party and a fascist labor party, the *Tohokai*, shows the extent to which organized labor and the "proletariat parties" had moved toward the right.

[43] M. Kohno, "Proletariat Movement," *Contemporary Japan*, Vol. V, March 1937, p. 583.

[44] Kohno, *Labour Movement in Japan*, p. 19. The figure usually given is 36. See below p. 53.

Though these returns may have been indicative of a dissatisfaction with the promises of the rightist as well as of the two
leading political parties, it should be remembered that nationalist doctrines had largely replaced socialist, even within the
Social Mass Party. Their attitude in. the emergency created
after July 1937 effectively checked strikes which had been on
the increase, and the repressive measures taken by the Government made any spontaneous labor movement impossible.[45]

Likewise, the fascist parties (*Kokumin Domei, Showakai,*
etc.) were unable to capture the support of the public, and
the only radical labor group, the Japan Proletarian Party (*Nippon Musanto*) elected only one member to Parliament, Mr.
Kanju Kato. This movement was effectively halted by his arrest in December 1937 along with "371 leftists, mostly members of the Japan Proletarian Party and the Japan National
Council of Labor Unions . . . suspected of working in accordance with Comintern's instructions for a revolution . . .[46]
Thus though the last election showed an increase in support
of the representative labor party, the party itself soon came
to acquiesce in principle with the Government's policies and
the radical movement practically disappeared with the increase in power of the patriotic movement.

Patriotic Societies

One of the most important features of the turbulent period
in Japan's history since 1931 has been the growth of patriotic
societies. Although no single society or group has had a monopoly of influence on Japan's policy, the various societies, whether
terroristic, ultra-patriotic or secret, have indirectly played a
leading role. There has been a gradual increase in the number
of these societies since the World War, a growth which is
closely correlated with the emergence of a national crisis. Of
about 235 organizations for "patriotic purposes" existing prior
to 1936,[47] nineteen had been organized in 1930, but the next
year the number jumped to forty-two, and a record of fifty-eight
was reached in 1932.[48]

[45] Mitsubishi Economic Research Bureau, *Japanese Trade & Industry,* Tokyo,
1936, p. 44; K. W. Colegrove, "Japan   as a Totalitarian State," *Amerasia,* Mar.
1938, p. 15.

[46] Colegrove, *Militarism in Japan,* p. 15; and *Contemporary Japan,* Mar. 1938,
p. 759.

[47] *Fortune,* September 1936, p. 120.

[48] Reed, *op. cit.,* p. 174. Of the ten leading rightist groups listed in another
source, four developed between 1932 and 1933, and among twenty-five others

Their most important objectives have been the exaltation of the Imperial House, the fostering of militarism either directly or indirectly, and the patriotic training of youth. Although they are supposedly spontaneous, private organizations, considerable official encouragement has been given them. One student of the modern Japanese spirit (*kokutai*) feels that:

> The significance of the role of patriotic societies in the life of the nation is easily exaggerated. Their prevalence may serve to unify and mobilize the nation, but the diversity of definition of national welfare sometimes suggests deleterious results. . . . The growth of patriotic societies becomes itself an index of the deficiency in patriotic sentiment or national immaturity.[49]

Before describing in detail some of these organizations, two important points should be noted. In the first place, although the terrorist activities of these numerous groups have received little check from the authorities no single dictator at the head of any party has emerged to direct policies as he pleased. In the second place, it is not of vital importance whether the various terrorist societies or ultra-nationalist patriots have had official backing for their various acts—a point which may never be definitely established. The important thing to note is that each time the public was terrorized and shocked by an attack on a leading government official, such as that on Hamaguchi in 1930 or the *coups d'état* in May 1932 and February 1936, the military leaders in power at the time were quick to take advantage of the situation and force concessions from the civil leaders, thus establishing themselves ever more securely.

The history of the rise of patriotic societies is more complicated than that of the labor and proletarian groups. In view of the unusually strong position of the military in recent times, by far the most important patriotic societies are those centering around the services. Of these the Ex-Service Men's Association (*Zaigo Gunjinkai*) is one of the oldest and most powerful. Originally formed in 1895, it is organized on military lines and has a membership of over 53,000 officers, 80,000 non-commissioned officers, and between 2½ and 3 million privates. Since its aim is the continuance of the spirit of soldiery and the military training of the people, it is natural that it should support

---

listed, seven were organized between 1930 and 1933. See Asahi Shimbun, *Gendai Seiji no Doko,* Tokyo, 1938, p. 237 *et seq.*

[49] Reed, *op. cit.*, p. 194.

actively the military program on the Asiatic continent. By 1932 it was controlled by the very group that was supporting this program: Generals Minami, Araki and Mazaki, and Admirals Kato, Nomura and Toeda.[50]

Far less powerful numerically, but much more vociferous and drastic in action, is the Imperial League of Young Officers (*Kokoku Seinen Shoko Domei*). Blatantly opposed to parliamentary government and always anxious to intimidate its enemies by direct action, it is a staunch supporter of expansion in China and increased defenses at home. Its early leaders dreamt of a Showa Restoration which would overthrow the power of the ordinary ministries, abolish the press and establish the dictatorship of the Emperor, with his chief advisers appointed from among its ranks. It has been involved in almost all the important conspiracies and is held responsible for such demonstrations as that against Dr. Kitokuro Ikki, the Minister of the Imperial Household in 1931, when he is reported to have advised "the Emperor contrary to the interests of the Army."[51]

Another type of patriotic group is the secret society open to civilians as well as to military men. One of the earliest of these was the Black Ocean Society (*Genyosha*) organized by Mr. Mitsuru Toyama in 1881 to develop Japan's continental policy. Shortly after its inception it was involved in terroristic activities and became a convenient tool for the execution of policies during the first Sino-Japanese War. Its work gave such men as Ryohei Uchida sufficient training to organize their own societies, like the Black Dragon Society (*Kokuryukai*).[52] This society, believing that "the Japanese are the leaders in the development of the Asiatic peoples," and that "all should become national soldiers, obeying the Emperor's orders and burning with a thirst for military exploits," naturally devoted its efforts to preparation for the Russo-Japanese War. Its activi-

[50] Colegrove, *Militarism in Japan*, p. 33 *et seq.*; and Tanin, *Militarism*, p. 63. Some authorities believe this society to be the most powerful influence in Japanese village life through its control over the Young Men's Association (*Seinendan*) and local educational policies.

[51] Colegrove, *Militarism in Japan*, p. 35 *et seq.* The Imperial League merged with the Chosen Men (*Seieikai*) in August 1931 and was then led by Majors Ishiwara and Hashimoto. It was involved in the following attempted *coups*: October 17, 1931, November 3, 1931, May 15, 1932 and February 26, 1936. Use of the term *Showa*, the name of the present reign, since 1926, indicates an analogy with the Meiji Restoration (1867-8).

[52] *Kokuryukai* is the Japanese equivalent for the name of the Amur River.

ties continue, however, down to the present. Of much more recent origin is the *Yusonsha*, a society whose members were inspired by the writings of Ikki Kita, and Shumei Okawa, former head of the economic research organization of the South Manchurian Railway. This group, which was formed in 1920, claimed that to be successful an aggressive foreign policy should be based on the removal of dissensions within the nation and the union of the people around the Emperor.[53]

The center of the reactionary movement after 1924 was the Society for the Foundation of the State (*Kokuhonsha*) which used the attempted assassination of the Crown Prince in 1924 to strengthen its status and to bolster up a new monarchist movement. Its chief efforts from that time until its dissolution in 1936 were directed to forcing the return of governmental power to the military and bureaucratic group. It maintained that "if we fail now to nourish and foster the national spirit, to strengthen the foundations of the nation, to promote virtue and wisdom together, and manifest the essence of *kokutai* (Japanese national polity), the future of the nation and of the people is uncertain." When it is realized that such men as Seihin Ikeda, former Minister of Finance, General Sadao Araki, former Minister of Education, and Baron Hiranuma, former Premier, were all among its directors, it is little wonder that recent Japanese politics have taken on a fascist aspect.[54]

The growth of patriotic societies in rural Japan indicates how easily the agricultural community can be influenced by group leaders. Of these the School of Love for the Native Soil (*Aikyo Juku*) of Kozaburo Tachibana and the League for Self-Government on the Countryside (*Nippon Sonjiha Domei*) of Nariaki Gondo are the most important. Both groups developed in the country and received moral as well as material support from members of some of the organizations already mentioned. Like those described above, their appeal lay in emphasis on reverence for the Emperor, denouncing the plutocracy, condemnation of the corruption of the large financiers and political parties, and the advocacy of Imperial socialism under the be-

[53] See Tanin, *op. cit.,* pp. 33, 41, 90; and Colegrove, *op. cit.,* p. 36. The name *Yusonsha* defies translation. It has been rendered as "The Society that Criticizes." The name is taken from a Buddhist phrase which indicates belief in the eternal existence of things even though death presupposes their non-existence.

[54] See *Gendai Seiji,* cited, p. 237; Reed, *op. cit.,* p. 173; and Colegrove, *Militarism in Japan,* cited, p. 31.

nign rule of the Emperor. Of the other numerous groups and societies,[55] one of the most interesting is the League of State Construction (*Kenkokukai*), originally organized in 1926 to observe the traditional rites of Empire Day. In an appeal to the Minister of Foreign Affairs in October 1933, it urged: (1) that an anti-Soviet war was the only means of saving the Empire from the disintegration due to the division of public opinion and the treacherous work of anti-national organizations; and (2) that Red Russia was the direct enemy of Japan and unless she were destroyed there would be no other prospect for the Empire but disintegration.[56] True to this tradition, seven members of the society visited the Soviet Embassy in Tokyo on July 19, 1938, in protest against the occupation of Changkufeng by Soviet troops. When they were refused an interview with the *charge d'affaires*, they scattered handbills demanding the immediate chastisement of Soviet Russia. Upon attempting a sit-down strike they were arrested by the police.[57]

The last example of these patriotic societies to be noted is the Young Men's Association (*Nippon Seinendan*), a nationwide organization, membership in which is open to any young men between 13-25 years, whose basic principles are "purity and genuineness." The members strive to enjoy hard work and expect to be men of self-reliance and originality. They love the State, abide by the fundamental principles of loyalty and filial piety and are ever ready to devote themselves to the service of the State and to make sacrifices in the interest of the nation.[58] Claiming a membership of about 2,400,000 in 1934, with a similar women's group of over 1½ million, the Association has 16,000 local units through which it can disseminate patriotism, or carry on its other activities. Since 1925 there has been a

[55] Such societies include the Women's Patriotic Society (*Aikoku Fujinkai*) with 1½ million membership in 1933, the Women's Defense Society (*Dai Nippon Kokubo Fujinkai*) organized in 1932, the League of Fidelity to the Emperor (*Kinno Remmei*) organized for the rural districts in 1924, the Society of Military Valor (*Dai Nippon Butokukai*) founded in 1897 and devoted solely to patriotic propaganda and the training of boys for the army, the Society of the Spirit of Great Japan (*Dai Nippon Kokusuikai*) organized in 1919 with the belief that the nation has a special mission to remedy the confusion in the Far East, and many others.

[56] O. Tanin and E. Yohan, *When Japan Goes to War*, New York, 1936, p. 261.

[57] *New York Times*, July 20, 1938.

[58] See Reed, *op. cit.*, p. 192 *et seq.* For a concise account of this Association see Tatsujiro Kumagai, *The Japan Young Men's Association*, Tokyo, June, 1935.

plenary annual conference, and staff members have received special training for inculcating in members the proper interpretation of the national policy. Since July 1937 special leaders have been attached to each local unit "to train members to be better qualified to meet the requirements of the times,"[59] each unit has been supplied with a radio set, and all have begun a drive for membership from among the 6,800,000 eligible young men. In connection with the present war, the potentialities of the Young Men's Association became apparent immediately. By February 1938 they had purchased four airplanes for the army and navy through collecting newspapers and magazines, while new aims have been adopted including assistance in the spiritual and industrial mobilization of the nation, the formation of Youth Volunteer Corps for the development of Manchuria and Mongolia, and the training of members in air defense and volunteer labor service. Ordinary activities include the publication of a monthly journal and bi-monthly newspaper. The importance of this association in the formation of a new patriotic movement is evident from the recent efforts of the new director, Mr. Masayasu Kozaka, a former prefectural governor, to make it follow the lines of national policy through strengthening the ties between the federation and its local organizations.[60]

Thus, even before the beginnings of expansion on the continent in 1931, numerous patriotic organizations were in existence. Members of these organizations frequently intimidated and even assassinated high Government officials, always in the name of patriotism, and many officials now in important positions seem to have been affiliated with them. The fact that their programs have varied widely on many points is less important than their common willingness to support any government or leader interested in expansion. Their ruthlessness and the diversity of their aims have made it personally dangerous for anyone to criticize the Government, and intimidation by the patriotic societies has been an important factor in recent years in making liberal leaders both inarticulate and impotent.

[59] Kumagai, *op. cit.*, p. 24.

[60] *Ibid.*, pp. 32, 41 *et seq.* Quite naturally the Young Men's Association was organized by men with very different motives than the leaders of the secret societies, but nonetheless, this society is a vital factor in strengthening patriotic feeling.

CHAPTER III

THE TREND TOWARD MILITARY FASCISM

Period of Direct Action—September 1931 to May 1932

The story of Japan's recent political development is largely one of a struggle for power among the leading groups. The military have been prominent in this struggle ever since the Imperial Restoration in 1868. They have opposed the capitalists with especial vehemence but also the monarchist-bureaucrats, the industrialists, the landowners and the political parties, although at no time was any of these groups completely independent of the others. Since the Manchurian venture the military groups have become increasingly important.[1]

Although an Imperial Rescript of the Emperor Meiji in 1882 forbade those in active military or naval service to participate in national politics, the change in the composition of the army has caused the edict to be interpreted broadly. As the prestige and power of the conservative army officers from western Japan (mostly Choshu) declined, there arose a group of militant young officers who came from the farming districts and were intent on reforming the country. Since 1927 over 20 per cent of the officers have come from the land. They have been determined to place "national defense on a broader basis," and to "stabilize the national livelihood." By their indiscriminate use of anti-capitalist slogans, together with their veneration of the position of the Emperor, they have been able to win sufficient support to dominate not only the army but also politics, and this has re-

[1] For those interested in detailed accounts of Japan since 1931, there is a wide choice available. Among them are: A. Morgan Young, *Imperial Japan, 1926-38,* New York, 1938. A leading foreign journalist in Japan for many years, Mr. Young has been able to give a detailed historical narrative of high value. T. A. Bisson, *Japan in China,* New York, 1938. A detailed account of events, 1931-8, by one who has long specialized on the Far East and returned to America just after the beginning of the war. William H. Chamberlin, *Japan Over Asia,* Boston, 1937. A general, objective survey of Japan's expansion by a keen observer and journalist of long experience in Russia and the Far East. The new edition of Chamberlin's work includes events up to April 1939. For a study of the role played by the military during the Restoration of 1868, see Norman, *op. cit.*

36

sulted in an active expansionist movement. Inspired by the more radical and outspoken of the older officers, such as Generals Muto, Araki, Mazaki and Hayashi,[2] they have implanted their ideals and aspirations in the whole nation.

There was a definite change, and in many respects a reversal, of Japan's policies both internal and external after 1931, although the possibility of such a change had been recognized prior to this time. In a speech before the divisional commanders in August 1931, General Jiro Minami, Minister of War, pointed to the gravity of the Manchurian problem and expressed regret that it might become "necessary for Japan reluctantly to have recourse to force," and suggested that they should "do their best to combat the increasing amount of propaganda derogatory to the military." Not only was this speech made public to prepare the people for any eventuality, but suggestions were made that the Korean garrison be increased to facilitate the movement of troops to Manchuria and to lessen the possibility of exciting the Powers by such movements. General Kazushige Ugaki, as Governor of Korea, asked for another division, and the General Staff advocated that the Manchurian garrison be increased to one division.[3] Thus the army was prepared to act.

The people likewise were far from satisfied with the government. Economically Japan was faced with a depression,[4] so that unemployment and social unrest provided fertile ground for any sort of fascist propaganda. The alliance of the political parties with the "politicians" led to continued corruption, which increased the gains of the capitalists and the hardships of the

[2] To control the policies of the army, it has been necessary to control the three key positions, those of Chief of General Staff, Inspector General of Education and Minister of War. All of these officers are appointed by the Emperor and are responsible to him, and up to the time of the present war, political moves within the army centered around appointments to these posts. The present situation is further complicated by the growing importance of the positions of Chief of the Kwantung Army, Chief of Forces in Central China, or Chief of Forces in South China. The appointment of General Toshizo Nishio as new Commander-in-Chief of the Japanese forces in China and Lieutenant-General Seishiro Itagaki as his chief-of-staff, is an attempt to eliminate friction among these groups. See H. M. G. Labatt-Simon, "The Japanese Military Machine," *Amerasia*, February 1938; *Trans-Pacific*, October 6, 1939.

[3] Sakuzo Yoshino, "Fascism in Japan," *Contemporary Japan*, Vol. I, 1932, p. 190. See also *Japan Weekly Chronicle*, Sept. 10, 1931, p. 322, where there is evidence of preparedness; also Sept. 24, 1931, p. 367.

[4] See below, p. 89.

peasants. Psychologically all that was needed was an appeal
to the innate patriotism of the Japanese to make them champion a policy of expansion rather than the less spectacular task
of improving their internal political and economic structure
by retrenchment entailing a possible loss of prestige.[5] Industrialization had played havoc with the old ideals, traditions,
and beliefs and neither the doctrines of Marx and Lenin nor a
westernized form of Christianity had been able to satisfy the
spiritual yearning of the people. They were questioning
"whether, after all, they would not be better served by a return to their old gods which . . . they had forsaken;"[6] and
this was exactly the path upon which the military leaders proposed to take them. After they had once launched on this program there was no turning back, and foreign utterances of
remonstrance and censure merely served to arouse national feeling. As soon as the nation as a whole felt itself misjudged and
ill-treated, it "tended more and more to prejudice its own case
in the eyes of the world by adopting an attitude of seemingly
stubborn aggressiveness."[7] The national reaction to the conflicts
in Manchuria and Shanghai in 1931 and 1933 appeared to
some to be as tremendous as it was during the first Sino-
Japanese War and the Russo-Japanese War. There was "an
abrupt awakening of patriotism among socialists and other
groups . . . to whom nationalism had been . . . anathema."[8]

The army was fully convinced of the necessity for control of
Manchuria, and in spite of the opposition of the Ministry of
Foreign Affairs and the Ministry of Finance, a state of national
crisis was proclaimed. During the first few months of this crisis,
Japan was faced with two formidable attempts at seizure of
the Government by force. The attempted *coups d'état* of October 17 and November 3, 1931, were both discovered by the
police, and investigations showed that secret societies and patriotic organizations were involved. The proposed *coup* of November 3 was the more important of the two. It centered around the
fascist section of the Social Democratic Party, under Katsumaro

[5] Yoshino, *op. cit.*, p. 193.

[6] M. S. Kennedy, "The Reactionary Movement of 1932," *Contemporary Japan*,
Vol. I, p. 632.

[7] *Ibid.*, p. 630.

[8] Choko Ikuta, "The Call of Fascism," *Chuo Koron*, April 1932, translated
in *Contemporary Japan*, Vol. I, p. 141.

Akamatsu, the Ex-Service Men's Organization, and the Society
for the Foundation of the State,[9] and had as its avowed purpose
the establishment of a military dictatorship. By December 11
the Wakatsuki Cabinet collapsed, and Mr. Inukai, the president of the rival Seiyukai Party since the death of Baron
Tanaka in 1929, formed a new cabinet the following day. The
gold embargo was immediately reimposed and inflation soon
replaced retrenchment.[10]

While the army was completing its campaign in Manchuria
in February 1932 and organizing the new Manchukuo Government in March, and while the navy was engaged in the
attack on Shanghai, the Seiyukai Party was gaining an overwhelming majority in the elections at home, so that when the
new Diet assembled there were 303 Seiyukai members and
144 Minseito, as opposed to 171 and 247, respectively, prior
to the elections.[11] The policy of direct action on the part of
ultra-patriotic individuals and groups continued. On February
9, 1932, Mr. Junnosuke Inouye, former Finance Minister and
campaign manager for the Minseito, and Baron Takuma Dan,
Chief Director of the Mitsui concerns, were murdered. These
assassinations, in which members of the Blood Brotherhood were
soon found to be implicated, were perpetrated in the name of
patriotism against men whom the assassins regarded as typical of
the politicians and capitalists who were bringing the country to
ruin.[12]

More important than either of these deeds themselves was
the impetus they gave to another attempt to seize the Government by force on May 15, 1932. This is usually referred to
simply as the May 15th Incident.[13] As already pointed out, it
involved the murder of Premier Inukai, attacks on other officials,
and the bombing of the Bank of Japan, the headquarters of the

[9] Bisson, *Japan in China*, p. 207. It has been maintained that General Sadao
Araki, the War Minister in the new cabinet, Prince Kanin, Chief of General
Staff, and Mr. Suzuki, the Minister of Justice, were all implicated, but if such
were the case, it had little effect on their holding their offices the next month.
See Tanin, *Militarism*, cited, p. 209 *et seq.* Naturally such an accusation is ex-
tremely difficult to prove.

[10] Young, *Imperial Japan*, p. 115. See also G. C. Allen, *Japanese Industry: Its
Recent Development and Present Condition*, International Secretariat, Institute
of Pacific Relations, New York, 1939.

[11] Bisson, "The Trend toward Dictatorship in Japan," *Foreign Policy Reports*,
Vol. X, No. 25, p. 318 *et seq.*; and Young, *op. cit.*, p. 127.

[12] Young, *op. cit.*, p. 118.

[13] See above, p. 18.

political parties, the Metropolitan Police Headquarters and electric power stations in Tokyo.

Deplorable as these acts may seem, they were in themselves not so important as the effect they had on Japan's future development.[14] They also reflected economic conditions which were far from encouraging. Japan's foreign trade had been halved during the period from 1929 to 1931. Farm income had been reduced by a third, and rural and industrial indebtedness amounted to more than the national income. Wages were cut, tenancy struggles were plentiful and the number of strikes reached a new high in 1932.[15]

General Araki and Events from May 1932 to February 1936

In spite of these alarming developments, those in authority were not willing to be intimidated or forced into unwarranted decisions. Prince Saionji was immediately consulted as to who should become premier. Both parties had lost considerably by the recent assassinations. The army had hoped for the appointment of Baron Hiranuma, leader in the Society of the Foundation of the State and an avowed fascist, who was at that time Vice-Chairman of the Privy Council. The Seiyukai, the majority party, had hoped that their new president, Dr. Kisaburo Suzuki, would receive that appointment, but Prince Saionji recommended a moderate, Admiral Makoto Saito, who formed a national cabinet, giving only five portfolios to party members. The most significant aspect of this government was the struggle between the armed services, typified by General Sadao Araki, the Minister of War, and the capitalists represented by General Korekiyo Takahashi, the Minister of Finance.[16] The latter strove valiantly to keep down the budget and thus check military expansion, but he was faced with insurmountable

[14] What is claimed to be a translation of part of a leaflet of the National Federation of Young Officers, without exact reference to the source quoted, will give some idea of the philosophy back of this *coup*. It states, "The Japanese army and navy, bound body and soul to the people, and to the tradition of Bushido, see with indignation the influence of commercial speculative circles growing to the detriment of national patriotism. The political parties, a common enemy of the nation, should be destroyed. The capitalists, with their arbitrary authority, should be killed. Under the leadership of the Emperor we must restore the true soul of our empire, and institute the principle of self government." Quoted in Tanin, *Militarism*, p. 202.

[15] Bisson, "Trend towards Dictatorship," p. 318.

[16] *Ibid.*, p. 322.

obstacles. For instance those tried for the recent political assassinations were given surprisingly light sentences considering the severity of their crimes, a fact which encouraged others contemplating similar action in the future. Dr. Koyama, the Minister of Justice, confessed "that he found it extremely difficult to punish a man for any act which he declared to have been performed from a patriotic motive."[17]

By quick decisive strokes the army was enhancing its reputation in Manchuria and at home. Manchuria was pacified, and Japan gave notice of her intention to withdraw from the League of Nations, March 27, 1933. Jehol and North China were invaded, the Tangku Truce, demilitarizing a large area south of the Great Wall, was signed on May 31, 1933, and Henry Pu Yi was declared Emperor of Manchukuo on March 1, 1934.[18] To carry on such activities a sudden rise in military expenditures was inevitable; they increased from ¥492.8 million in 1930 to ¥851.8 million in 1933, and in 1934 military expenditures totaling ¥937.3 million comprised 43.7 per cent of the entire budget. In this connection, it appears that the Diet had little opportunity for a real discussion of fundamental issues. According to a contemporary newspaper report, whenever the question of national financial policy was raised in the Diet, the ministers replied that the time was not opportune for a frank discussion of it. Parliament, which was supposed to represent the people, was likewise ignored in regard to Japan's policy toward the League of Nations, and treated as if its main function was to listen. Even one of Japan's reactionary papers, commenting on the responses of the Finance Minister and the Premier to inquiries as to why the services needed ¥900,000-000 when there was a deficit in the new budget of a billion yen, declared that "The very elusiveness of their replies leads one to doubt that they themselves know the why and wherefore of the war-like appropriations."[19] The War Minister, General Araki, remarked that the appropriations would increase in the

[17] The slayer of Hamaguchi was sentenced to death in February, only to have his sentenced commuted in February 1934. The eleven cadets who killed Premier Inukai were given four years, but became heroes as a result. Others received fifteen years, but many were released in 1936. See also Young, op. cit., p. 175.

[18] For a detailed analysis of these events, see Bisson, Japan in China, p. 40 et seq.

[19] Osaka Mainichi, February 2, 1933, quoted in Pacific Affairs, Vol. VI, 1933, pp. 110-11.

future and the reasons were none of the outsiders' business. The Navy Minister concurred in this, but made no further remark. In the end, the Diet approved the budget.

It is significant that with military success abroad and apparent Government support at home the Foreign Office spokesman, Mr. Amau, should have issued the following statement in April 1934:

> Accordingly, unification of China, preservation of her territorial integrity, as well as restoration of order in that country, are most ardently desired by Japan. History shows that these can be attained through no other means than the awakening and the voluntary efforts of China herself.
>
> We oppose therefore any attempt on the part of China to avail herself of the influence of any other country in order to resist Japan; we also oppose any action taken by China, calculated to play one Power against another. Any joint operations undertaken by foreign Powers, even in the name of technical or financial assistance, at this particular moment after the Manchurian and Shanghai Incidents, are bound to acquire political significance. Undertakings of such nature, if carried through to the end, must give rise to complications that might eventually necessitate discussions of problems like fixing spheres of influence or even international control or division for China, which would be the greatest possible misfortune for China and at the same time would have the most serious repercussion upon Japan and East Asia.
>
> Japan, therefore, must object to such undertakings as a matter of principle, although she will not find it necessary to interfere with any foreign country negotiating individually with China on questions of finance or trade, as long as such negotiations benefit China and are not detrimental to the maintenance of peace in the Far East.
>
> However, supplying China with war planes, building aerodromes in China and detailing military instructors or military advisers to China, or contracting a loan to provide funds for political uses, would obviously tend to alienate the friendly relations between Japan and China and other countries and to disturb peace and order in East Asia. Japan will oppose such projects.
>
> The foregoing attitude of Japan should be clear from the policies she has pursued in the past, but on account of the fact that positive movements for joint action in China by foreign Powers, under one pretext or another, are reported to be on foot, it is deemed not inappropriate to reiterate her policy.[20]

Nowhere is the spirit of this pronouncement and the new trend of the times better exemplified than in the figure of General Sadao Araki. Born in 1877 of humble parentage, he worked in a soy-bean sauce factory, but later became president of the Military Academy and War Minister from 1931 to Janu-

[20] Quoted in *The China Year Book, 1934*, pp. 725-6.

ary 1934. Although one of a score of lieutenant-generals, he became the idol of the army, for his motives were pure, his personal habits simple, and he was at heart a soldier. Above all, he was devoted to the Imperial Way, *Kodo*, and this devotion soon resulted in his becoming the spiritual leader of a new Japan.[21] True, he resigned from the Ministry of War in January 1934, to be succeeded by the less vociferous General Senjuro Hayashi, but his influence as Minister of War and that of his friend, General Mazaki, who was Inspector-General of Education until his resignation under pressure in November 1934, had left an indelible imprint on Japan. When the Saito Cabinet was forced to resign in July 1934 because of a scandal connected with one of its ministers, the radical nationalists clamored for Hiranuma. Admiral Keisuke Okada, a moderate, was appointed, but the general policy remained the same. General Araki and his group propagandized the public with their beliefs and hopes through a series of Army pamphlets.

These pamphlets marked the culmination of a chain of events begun in the summer of 1931. They first appeared in March 1934 and emphasized the necessity of more adequate defense, commented on the general principles underlying it and described specific aspects of defense in Japan. They maintained, for instance, that the air forces of the Soviet Union and the United States were a menace which should be overcome by an increase in Japanese aerial armaments. Moreover, the unstable balance of power in Europe and its various political theories threatened Japan, and broad economic and social mobilization of the nation was essential for proper preparation against war.[22] In October there appeared one of the most important of these entitled "Principles of National Defense and a Plea for its Strengthening." The pamphlets created the idea of the "1936 crisis." The soul of Japan was praised and the Japanese were said to be destined to bring order and peace to the continent of Asia through the workings of the Imperial Way. War, the father of Creation, was not to be condemned but encouraged, since rivalry for supremacy does for the state what struggling against adversity does for the individual. The whole nation should be mobilized for defense and a new régime of

[21] Colegrove, *Militarism,* p. 45 and below p. 115.
[22] For accounts of these pamphlets, see Colegrove, *op. cit.;* and Colegrove, "Military Propaganda in Japan," *Amerasia,* April 1937, p. 63 *et seq.*

social justice promoted which would provide higher wages and rural relief.[23] Other pamphlets emphasized the necessity of beginning every study with the consciousness that "I am a Japanese," because, they said, Japan had been insulted and the Japanese had forgotten their national pride.

Not only in order to work out protective measures with respect to Manchuria and Mongolia, but also to show the world our brilliant essence, it is necessary for us that the entire nation be awakened to the convictions and ideals of the Imperial Army so that the people will have the determination to go in for ever bigger aims avoiding individual pragmatic ideas.[24]

The economic development of the continent of Asia was urged, and the whole expansionist program was given the necessary philosophical and religious justification. The three sacred Imperial treasures were used as symbols not only of the right of the Emperor to rule, but also of high ideals. The mirror represented uprightness, the jewels compassion, and the sword bravery, all of which could be realized under the proposed plan of national expansion.[25] In fine, a crisis was at hand. Japan must perform her mission in Asia and must protect herself from within against the enemies, communism and capitalism, by a powerful nationalistic government; she must be prepared for any enemies from without by relentlessly increasing her military appropriations.

Although present political events in the Orient reveal the manner in which many of these principles have prevailed, it must not be forgotten that dissension regarding them existed even within the army. Generals Araki and Mazaki and their fellow-advocates of an "Imperial Way" were not completely

[23] See *Kokubo no Hongi*, "Fundamental Principles of National Defense and a Plea for its Strengthening," War Ministry, Tokyo, 1934.

[24] Quoted from "Problems Facing Japan in the Era of Showa," War Ministry, Tokyo, 1934, in Tanin, *Militarism*, p. 297 *et seq.* For a pamphlet on the nurturing of the spirit of the soldiers see "Pflege des Soldatengeistes in der Kaiserlich-Japanischen Wehrmacht," *Deutsche Gesellschaft für Natur und Völkerkunde Ostasiens*, Vol. 28, War Ministry, Tokyo, 1939.

[25] Kiyoshi Hiraizumi, *Bushido no Fukkatsu*, Tokyo, 1933, p. 252. Professor Hiraizumi is professor of medieval Japanese history in Tokyo Imperial University. Other sources of inspiration for the army pamphlets are: Mr. Masaatsu Yasuoka, a sociologist and translator of Spengler's *Decline of the West*; Mr. Kamekichi Takahashi, an economist; Mr. Seiichi Kojima, who visited Manchuria in 1931 and was converted to expansionism; members of the Imperial Young Officers' League, and others. Many of the ideas expressed in these pamphlets are similar to those which motivated the officers and others taking part in the political assassinations in February and May 1932.

persona grata with the high command. Both had been forced
to retire from the two most important military posts as a result
of a purge conducted by General Hayashi with the assistance of
Major-General Nagata, Director of the Military Affairs Bureau.
These "reforms" were rudely interrupted by the resignation of
General Hayashi, then Minister of War, who felt responsible for
the lack of discipline within the army, which had become evident when Lieutenant-Colonel Aizawa took it upon himself to
ask his superior, Nagata, to resign. When the only answer to this
request was that Aizawa was ordered transferred to Formosa,
he murdered Nagata in an effort to rid the army of what he believed to be "degenerate" elements.[26]

Politically Japan was in a turmoil as well. The Okada Cabinet
was insecure and the Seiyukai party forced a dissolution of the
Diet in January 1936. The elections of February were a censure
by the people of the extreme nationalists but no candidate
came out violently against the Government's China policy. All
of the nationalistic parties lost, the Minseito became the leading
party, the Social Mass Party increased its representation from
three to eighteen, and the local proletarians won three seats.
The labor representatives received double the votes cast in
1932.[27] Unless they were to admit defeat, the extreme elements
in the army were likely to take some drastic action. This was all
the more probable since these elements had been acting very
arbitrarily for several months.

Extreme Violence and Opposition, February 1936 to April 1937

The most violent of all the attempted *coups d'état* in recent
years was that perpetrated by Captain Teruzo Ando, his fellow-
officers and men early on the morning of February 26, 1936.
The reverses which the ultra-nationalistic groups had just re-

[26] Colegrove, *Militarism*, p. 56; Young, *Imperial Japan*, p. 273 *et seq.*; and
Fahs, *op. cit.*

[27] *Japan Year Book 1937*, p. 134; *Japan Weekly Chronicle*, February 27, 1936,
p. 252, and March 5, 1936, p. 289. The elections were as follows:

	Jan. 1936	Elected	Change
Minseito	127	205	+78
Seiyukai	242	174	−68
Showakai (Nationalist)	24	20	− 4
Kokumin Domei (Nationalist)	20	15	− 5
Social Mass Party (Shakai Taishuto)	3	18	+15
Independent	11	25	+14
Other Parties	0	9	+ 9

ceived at the elections, revealing the people's dissatisfaction with a continued expansionist policy, and the purge within the army instigated by General Hayashi as War Minister, were some of the forces working to create unrest and discontent among various elements in the army. That there were hard feelings was amply shown by Colonel Aizawa's murder of Major-General Nagata. On February 25 General Mazaki, whose removal from the position of Inspector-General of Military Education, had been one of the motives for the murder,[28] was summoned to the court-martial of Aizawa, but refused to speak. The court-martial adjourned and next morning groups of about thirty soldiers set out on their murderous task. Prince Saionji, the *Genro*, and Count Makino, former Lord-Keeper of the Privy-Seal, were outside Tokyo and, learning of the impending danger, escaped. Other staunch supporters of parliamentary government and opponents of the aggressive designs of the army were less fortunate. Finance Minister Korekiyo Takahashi, who had continually opposed increased appropriations for the services, when expenditures greatly exceeded revenue, was ruthlessly murdered. The new Inspector-General of Military Education appointed after Mazaki resigned, Lieutenant-General Jotaro Watanabe, was killed, as was Admiral Makoto Saito, Lord-Keeper of the Privy-Seal. The Grand Chamberlain, Admiral Kantaro Suzuki, was severely wounded. The Premier's official residence was entered and his brother-in-law, Colonel Denzo Matsuo, was killed by mistake.[29] In spite of these murders, the occupation by the insurgents of the Police Headquarters, the War Ministry and the new Diet Building and their stubborn refusal to surrender for three days, the *coup* failed. Martial law, proclaimed on February 27, was continued in Tokyo and the army issued official explanations and assurances that discipline had been restored.

Naturally the repercussions of this event were tremendous. The extremist group of army officers resigned from the Supreme Command, probably as a result of a reprimand by the Emperor to General Mazaki. The Okada Cabinet fell. Mr. Koki Hirota was asked to form a cabinet when Prince Fumimaro Konoye

[28] *Japan Weekly Chronicle*, March 5, 1936, p. 383 *et seq.*; and Young, *Imperial Japan*, p. 276. Mr. Young has described in a vivid manner events centering around February 26, 1936, pp. 268-85.

[29] Young, *op. cit.*, p. 276 *et seq.*

refused. The task before Premier Hirota was a difficult one. He had been thwarted in his attempt to place more moderate statesmen in his cabinet by the refusal of General Terauchi to serve as Minister of War.[30] The Premier thus was virtually at the mercy of the army since it had vetoed his choice of ministers and had directed him to choose Dr. Eiichi Baba, former governor of the Hypothec Bank, as Finance Minister.[31]

After this, the army rested on its laurels and created the impression that not only had it saved the country from the dangers of revolt (even against its own members) but that it had no further intentions of centralizing power in its own hands. A liberal independent journal seems to have taken them at their word and commented editorially:

> While it is true that Mr. Hirota made a certain revision of his Cabinet program on the advice of General Terauchi, to brand the General's action as military meddling shows lack of a correct conception of the circumstances. It would be rash to conclude that this conceded fact presages the Hirota government's taking orders from the Army so as to become its puppet. . . . Granted, that the Army lorded it over the Cabinet, it is entirely unthinkable that social and economic changes of any magnitude might occur. Moreover, neither is the Army equal to such a task nor has it the intention to undertake it.[32]

Other signs showed distinctly that the extremists had overplayed their hands. Finance Minister Baba's pronouncement that a new financial policy would be inaugurated had grave repercussions, but his policy of increased national expenditure to develop Manchuria and strengthen national defense was adopted. The Emperor, in his address to the Diet in May, expressed indignation over the Incident of February 26 in the following terms: "We regret the outbreak of the recent incident in Tokyo. It is expected of our faithful subjects that they will unite as one government and people, civilians and military, in order to promote the development of the national fortunes." On May 7 Mr. Takao Saito, a member of the Minseito, spoke

[30] For instance, the Minseito Party was to be represented by Mr. Kawasaki as Home Minister, but this post went to Mr. Keinosuke Ushio, a bureaucrat. Mr. Ohara, Minister of Justice, was unacceptable because he had been too lenient at the trial of Dr. Minobe.

[31] *Japan Weekly Chronicle*, March 12, 1936, p. 323. Particular objections were raised to Hirota's proposals of Mr. Shigeru Yoshida, former ambassador to Italy, as Foreign Minister, and Mr. Hiroshi Shimomura, vice-president of the *Asahi*, as another minister.

[32] *Oriental Economist*, April 1936, p. 213.

before an extremely attentive House on the subject of the recent *coup*. In part he said:

> I want to express the sentiments of the whole nation. . . . There is a limit to the patience of the nation . . . but . . . frankly . . . the people are indignant and you (the Minister of War) should take steps to rectify this condition in the Army.[33]

To this reprimand, General Terauchi merely answered that he agreed with Mr. Saito's statement, and his word was partially kept in July when thirteen former army officers who had led the revolt were executed.

After this verdict, the army again felt it necessary to explain its position and to maintain that the ideas of the insurgents were in conflict with the sound ideas of the majority of the army and navy.[34] Whether such was really the case is unimportant in view of the fact that their four basic principles—Vindication of the national polity (*Kokutai*), stabilization of the livelihood of the people, reform of foreign policy and strengthening of national defense—were in reality advocated by the Hirota Government and by now have become basic tenets of Japanese policy. The appointments made after the various assassinations had little fundamental effect on policies. Although General Minami was recalled from his duties as head of the Kwantung Army and Ambassador to Manchukuo, he was transferred to the Supreme War Council. His post in Manchuria was filled by General Kenkichi Ueda.[35]

[33] *Problems of the Pacific, 1936,* p. 92. For an account of the shift in financial policies of Takahashi and Baba, see Allen, *Japanese Industry,* cited, Chapter VI.

[34] The official War Office report of July 6, 1936, remarked: "The insurgents thought the time had arrived when the country must devise measures for development of national fortunes by enhancing the national spirit, replenishing national defense measures and armaments and stabilizing the national life. . . . They were of the opinion that the prerogatives of the Supreme Command had been violated when the London Naval Treaty was concluded. They attributed this state of affairs to insincerity on the part of the statesmen close to the Throne, the bureaucrats, the military clique, the political parties and the financial clique, toward the principles of national structure. They thought that to give luster to the real nature of the constitution it was necessary to renovate the nation by striking at the so-called privileged classes. To strike at the senior statesmen, it would be necessary to transcend the Constitution and use part of the army in direct action. They thought this a popular way to cope with the existing emergency. By so acting they planned to clarify the national polity, replenish the national defense, and stabilize national living. They intended in this manner to urge high elements in the army to bring about the Showa Restoration." See Reed, *op. cit.,* p. 158 *et seq.*

[35] Colegrove, *Militarism,* p. 57; and *Japan Weekly Chronicle,* March 26, 1936, p. 378.

Admiral Saito had been succeeded by Mr. Kurahei Yuasa as Lord-Keeper of the Privy-Seal, and Mr. Tsuneo Matsudaira was the new minister of the Imperial Household, but any victory which this might indicate for the moderates was more than offset by Baron Hiranuma's succession to the presidency of the Privy Council. Above all, though discipline within the army had broken down over specific methods of government, everyone knew that unity of action against the outside world was not threatened in the slightest. Owing in large measure to the political views of the Emperor, the high officials surrounding him and the distrust of the army still prevalent among the bourgeois groups and masses, a totalitarian state was temporarily avoided, but a glance at the increasing military appropriations shows the new grip the services were getting on the vital organs of the State.[36]

On October 9, 1936, a plan for government reform in the form of a joint appeal by the army and navy was handed to Premier Hirota. This emphasized the necessity for a complete renovation of all administrative bodies and the formation of a central organ directly under the prime minister which should control all important government problems. The Foreign Minister was asked to take over the responsibilities of the Overseas Minister. Commerce, Industry and Agriculture were to be under a single portfolio, and the Department of Education was to have surveillance over shrines. Communications were to be unified. Other proposals called for restrictions on the electorate, and more severe laws governing the Diet, especially the Lower House. Quite naturally these reforms were not received enthusiastically by the Government.[37]

When questioned by his opponents, General Terauchi as War Minister denied the truth of reports of such a plan. At a committee meeting of the Parliamentary System Investigation Commission on December 2, 1936, he stated:

The Army has nothing to do with the press report . . . on the parliamentary system alleged to have emanated from military sources. That report was a magnified account of the personal view expressed by a party working in the military affairs bureau of the War Department. This man has since been properly punished. . . . Some are engaged in spreading the rumor that the Army is bent upon a revision of the Constitution or the abolition

[36] See below, p. 81.
[37] *Gendai Seiji,* p. 182; and *Japan Weekly Chronicle,* October 8, 1936, p. 452.

of the Diet, which is, of course, absolutely without foundation. . . . The Army is opposed to the operation of the parliamentary institution along democratic ideas of the Western type. It is hoped that the Diet and the Election Laws will be so amended that fair popular opinion and national intellectual faculties shall be given full opportunity for their demonstration. It is keenly desired that a constitutional Government based on a Constitution which is all our own be allowed to develop. The law prohibits soldiers in the active service from concerning themselves in politics and such an excursion cannot, of course, be tolerated.[38]

Other conditions were far from encouraging. The ambassador to China, Mr. Kawagoe, had been rebuffed in his talks with Generalissimo Chiang Kai-shek. The Mongolian uprising in Suiyuan, which had enjoyed Japanese support, had resulted in failure. No sooner had the Hirota Government sponsored the signing of the Anti-Comintern Pact with Germany in November than criticism immediately arose against it. At home, Mr. Baba introduced new taxation measures to supplement revenue. These took the form of sales taxes, an increase in the prices of sugar and tobacco, higher postal charges, etc.[39] They affected the people in the lower income brackets most seriously.

The budget showed a deficit of ¥806,000,000; so a sharp rise in prices was not surprising. The wholesale price index for January 1937 had risen 8.6 per cent above that for December 1936 and 21.6 per cent above that of January 1936. Retail prices had risen 2.26 per cent in a month. The military were doing all in their power, in spite of the soporific utterances of General Terauchi, to increase armaments and mobilize financial resources on their side.[40] Heavy industries had received government patronage and were gaining in importance at the expense of the light industries, principally textiles, owned by the Osaka groups which supported a liberal policy.[41] Some of the old industrialists were profiting from this new swing toward increased armaments production, but the new Japan Production Company (Nippon Sangyo Kabushiki Kaisha) of Mr. Aikawa, with ¥225 million capital, was favorably treated by the

[38] Quoted in *Oriental Economist,* December 1936, p. 751.

[39] Bisson, *Japan in China,* cited, p. 233.

[40] *Ibid.,* p. 240 *et seq.*

[41] In 1931, textiles amounted to 37.7 per cent of the total manufactured products; heavy industries and chemicals only 33.7 per cent. In 1935 with production increased by over 100 per cent, textiles were 30.9 per cent, heavy industries and chemicals 47.2 per cent. See A. Bisson, "Japan's Home Front," *Foreign Policy Report,* Vol. XIV, No. 12, p. 137.

authorities and was challenging the old, established firms like the Mitsui and Mitsubishi.[42]

Interpellations again broke out in the Diet, led by Mr. Kunimatsu Hamada, a Seiyukai member. On January 21, 1937, he assailed the Minister of War by saying that dictatorial political ideology was an undercurrent of the talk and movements of a part of the military circle. This caused General Terauchi to attempt to dissolve parliament, but the Diet was prorogued for two days. Then the War Minister resigned, causing the downfall of Premier Hirota.[43]

The next few days clearly showed who were in control of the nation. When on January 25 General Kazushige Ugaki, former Governor-General of Korea, was requested to form a cabinet, he could find no one both willing and eligible to fill the post of Minister of War, for his selection was rigorously opposed by Prince Kanin, the Chief of Staff, General Terauchi and General Sugiyama, Inspector-General of Education, on the grounds that army discipline could not be restored were he to form a government. Regretfully he gave up his attempts and remarked that he feared Japan was at last standing at the crossroads between fascism and parliamentary politics. General Senjiro Hayashi was finally selected as Premier on January 29, and no party ministers were allowed to retain their party affiliations while in his cabinet. General Sugiyama, former Inspector-General, changed places with General Terauchi, former War Minister, a week after the cabinet was formed. The increasingly close alliance between the industrialists and the Government was revealed through the appointment of Mr. Toyotaro Yuki, former president of the Industrial Bank and the Japanese Chamber of Commerce, as Finance Minister, and the consequent appointment of Mr. Seihin Ikeda, former director of the Mitsui interests, as Governor of the Bank of Japan. This was done, among other reasons, to facilitate the utilization of the large credits of the bank for the expansion of heavy industries.[44] Thus not only had the army forced the resignation of one ministry, but it had checked the formation of another, and the

---

[42] Bisson, *Japan in China*, p. 238.

[43] *Japan Year Book, 1938-9*, p. 141 *et seq.*

[44] *Ibid.*, p. 143 *et seq.*; and *Japan Weekly Chronicle*, February 11, 1937, p. 170. For further appointments of Ikeda and Yuki see below pp. 57 and 65.

Terauchi-Sugiyama clique had been able to select its own premier.

Through the reduction of the budget by ¥224 million at the expense of non-service ministries such as agriculture, the elimination of taxes on business, and the shipment of gold abroad, business confidence was restored. Out of a total budget of ¥2,804,000,000, the services were promised slightly over 50 per cent. With the constant threat of dissolution before it, the Diet passed the Yuki budget, and immediately thereafter (April 1937) the Diet was dissolved. Having obtained a new budget, the authorities were willing to risk an election in the face of increasing opposition. Mr. Yukio Ozaki, Japan's most courageous liberal, had addressed a questionnaire to the cabinet in March demanding an explanation of the facts which prevented General Ugaki from forming a government, and other pertinent questions concerning the role the army was playing in politics.[45] Likewise, an economic mission to China, under the leadership of Mr. Konji Kodama, former president of the Yokohama Specie Bank, had failed to win Chinese friendship by an offer to return to China the silver held by Japanese banks. Foreign Minister N. Sato had remarked that war could be averted with China if Japan treated her as an equal, but he was forced to "supplement his somewhat inadequate remarks," and this amounted to a recantation.

The exact reasons for Hayashi's dissolution of the Diet are

[45] Bisson, *Japan in China*, p. 252 *et seq*. The Government explained the dissolution as follows:

"To cope with prevailing conditions at home and abroad, surmount the current difficulties and promote the national fortunes, cooperation between the Government and the people in the proper sense is absolutely essential. Thus the Cabinet, though it had just been formed, sought in the present session of the Diet the passage of many bills in all sincerity. The manner in which the Lower House has discussed these bills, however, has been extremely lacking in earnest, with the result that proceedings have been blocked with regard to important bills having the greatest bearing on national defense and stabilization of the living of the people, urgent business held up and doubts aroused as to whether parliamentary discussion could be carried on further in the way required by the seriousness of the prevailing situation.

"We therefore saw much reason in the clamour for renovation of the Diet. In the hope of appealing to the just conscience of the people, submitting to the will of the people and making manifest the principles of the constitutional government of Japan, and at the same time in expectation of sound political awakening on the part of the people and cooperation between them and the Government in surmounting the present serious situation, we have petitioned the Throne for dissolution of the House of Representatives." Quoted from *Japan Year Book 1938-9*, p. 145.

difficult to determine. Apparently dissension existed within the
cabinet over the question of the treatment the political parties
should receive at the hands of the Government. Possibly
Hayashi thought an election would discipline them. In any
case, he adopted the following election slogans: "The vote cast
with understanding serves the situation," "The correct appre-
ciation of the situation helps Japan forward," and "Public service at (sic) self-sacrifice is the keynote of politics."[46] These gen-
eralities throw little light on his real motives. In any case, the
two leading parties, the Seiyukai and Minseito, fearing that
their very existence was challenged, made common cause against
Hayashi and fascism.[47] The result was an overwhelming defeat
for General Hayashi and his supporters, for the Cabinet won
a bare fifty seats out of a total of 466.[48] The Minseito was in the
lead, but the most surprising aspect of the election was the fact
that the Social Mass Party had increased its representation in
Parliament from 18 to 36. In spite of this affront, and continued,
united opposition from the parties, the Government refused to
resign. Finally, criticized by Prince Konoye, then president of
the House of Peers, confronted with a hostile Privy Council
and even with opposition from some of his cabinet colleagues,
Premier Hayashi and his Cabinet resigned at the end of May
1937. Prince Fumimaro Konoye then formed a cabinet which
guided Japan through the turbulent days ahead.

*Demise of the Liberals and Ascendancy of New Bureaucrats in
    Konoye Cabinet*

The new Government, formed by Prince Fumimaro Konoye,
was further detached from the parties than any previous ones.
Messrs. Ryutaro Nagai and Chikuhei Nakajima were leaders
of the Minseito and Seiyukai, respectively, but filled the posts
of Ministers of Communications and Railways not as party men
but as individuals. The leader of the bureaucrats, Mr. Koki
Hirota, was the new Foreign Minister. Former Finance Minister Baba became Home Minister and two new bureaucrats,
both largely under the influence of the military, Mr. Okinori

[46] *Japan Weekly Chronicle,* April 15, 1937, p. 449.

[47] Iizawa, *Politics,* cited, p. 42.

[48] As a result of the elections the party strength in the Lower House was as
follows: Minseito 179, Seiyukai 175, Social Mass 36, Showakai 18, Kokumin
Domei 11, Tohokai 11, Independents and others 36. See *Japan Year Book
1938-9,* p. 145. For returns of the previous elections see above p. 45, note 27.

Kaya and Mr. Shinji Yoshino, occupied the positions of Finance
Minister and Minister of Commerce and Industry. The military
extremists were well satisfied with the appointments of General
Hajime Sugiyama as War Minister and Admiral Mitsumasa
Yonai as Navy Minister. They were in an even stronger position
after December when Admiral Suetsugu, an ardent nationalist,
succeded Mr. Baba as Home Minister. Mr. Suehiko Shiono, a
friend of nationalist Baron Hiranuma, was the Minister of
Justice. Thus the new cabinet became extremely nationalistic
as well as bureaucratic and its policy was dictated almost entirely by the events that took place on the continent in July
1937. Not only were the potentially liberal members of the
cabinet successfully silenced by new military operations in
China, but the cabinet sponsored a new and more intense program of unification and centralization. Independent liberals,
such as Yukio Ozaki, were impotent and Japan slowly drifted
into a state of war psychology under which all activities were
directed toward a speedy and successful termination of the
struggle.[49]

The situation was described by Mr. Toshio Shiratori, former
ambassador to Italy, in the following terms:

> The tide has turned against that liberalism and democracy that once
> swept over the nation. The once widely accepted theory of government
> which sees in parliament the real center of power now has been com-
> pletely rejected and the country is fast reverting to totalitarianism, which
> has been the fundamental principle of Japan's national life for the past
> thirty centuries."[50]

Though there had been certain external modifications of governmental forms under the influence of political theories imported from abroad, Japan, he said, had followed no other
principle since the beginning of history; it was a thing eternal
and immutable to the Japanese. "For Oriental nations, the
question is not one of making a new choice but of rediscovering
themselves and returning to their ancient faith . . . it makes
our hearts warm to see ideas that have influenced our races for
centuries in the past embodied in the systems of modern states

[49] Prince Konoye's appointment of parliamentary vice-ministers and councillors
from among party men showed his desire to eliminate internal friction, but the
outbreak of hostilities forced his cabinet to become a strong national one.

[50] T. Shiratori, "Fascism vs. the Popular Front," *Contemporary Japan*, March
1938, Vol. VI, p. 582.

of Europe."[51] But before the country had completely "reverted
to totalitarianism," much remained to be done in changing the
functions of the existing forms of government and in the passage and application of social, political and economic control
measures. That these changes should be inaugurated was due
in no small measure to the unrivaled position of power which
the military had reached in Japan's political structure during
the dramatic months after September 1931.

[51] *Ibid.*, pp. 585, 587, 589.

CHAPTER IV

RECENT LEGISLATION AND NEW ADMINISTRATIVE ORGANS

Recent Events

An unmistakable trend toward centralization of power had developed. The military were quick to profit from the general political disturbance following every national crisis, and gradually they acquired more power. After the outbreak of hostilities in China in July 1937, the extremists had even better chances to dictate policy, and the Konoye Cabinet found itself faced with the task of creating a strong nationalized state to meet the new crisis. The movement for a centralized state was greatly accelerated by the new hostilities, and the leaders quickly inaugurated measures which placed Japan on a war-time basis within a year.[1]

Inasmuch as large quantities of war supplies were immediately required for the army and navy, the Industry Mobilization Law, originally promulgated on April 17, 1918, was enacted on September 10, 1937. By this enactment the Government was empowered to take the necessary measures for efficient operation of the more important industries. Factories manufacturing or repairing articles of war and those producing raw materials or fuel for such factories were liable to Government control. Property could be confiscated, the import or export of raw materials and fuel could be controlled, and requisition could be made of materials as well as labor.[2] As this law also provided for the effective operation of these provisions, the Government was in a far stronger position than at any other time since the World War. To supplement this measure, various laws, such as those restricting the transport of horses, and the reduction, exemption and postponement of the payment of taxes for soldiers

[1] *Tokyo Gazette,* No. 4, October 1937, p. 9.
[2] *Tokyo Gazette,* No. 3, September 1937, p. 48, and Tanin, *When Japan Goes to War,* cited, p. 125 *et seq.* for an analysis of the provisions of this law.

and other persons serving in the war, were enacted. The movement toward national mobilization was under way.

Cabinet Planning Board

The successful execution of the Munitions Industry Mobilization Law was facilitated by the existence of three policy-making commissions which had been appointed by, and were the heritage of, the nationalist cabinet of General Hayashi. The first of these, the Price Policy Commission, devised remedies for the unusual rise of commodity prices and advised the Konoye Cabinet to adopt a stricter law of industrial control than the Principal Industries Control Law under which the cartels were operating.[3] The second commission was that of Education and Culture, whose task was to study matters relating to the thorough diffusion of the concept of Japanese national polity (*kokutai*) and the promotion of the national spirit in general. And the third was the Cabinet Planning Board which had been established by General Hayashi following the failure of the Board of General Affairs to materialize under the Hirota Ministry. Headed by Mr. Toyotaro Yuki, Finance Minister in the Hayashi Cabinet, this new board was promulgated by Imperial Ordinance on May 14, 1937. It consisted of twenty full-time councillors, with fifteen assistants and permanent advisers appointed from among officials of other bureaus of the Government. Acting largely as a coordinating and directing agent, and directly attached to the cabinet, it transcended all departments and had power to decide the urgency, importance, and priority of the proposals and claims made by the various departments. Furthermore, as evidenced by the fact that it was responsible for the authorship of the National Mobilization Law enacted March 16, 1938, it had the power to prepare bills for submission to the Diet, as well as to make recommendations on economic matters. It was, in fact, an extremely effective organization for the formation of a unified national policy.

Following the inauguration of the Konoye Cabinet, Mr. Koki Hirota succeeded Mr. Yuki as Chairman of the Board, so that by the beginning of hostilities in July 1937 an organization already existed to prevent any departmental suggestions from running counter to a unified national policy or those of any minister from being in conflict with the Prime Minister or his

[3] *Far Eastern Survey,* Vol. VI, August 4, 1937, p. 184. See also Fahs, *op. cit.,* p. 65.

most influential adviser.[4] The Board was closely related to the
Central Economic Council established by Imperial Ordinance
on July 1 to serve the Prime Minister by investigating and study-
ing the policies which he referred to it, such as the coordination
of economic measures and their execution in reference to the
Japanese Empire as a whole. The president of the Central Economic Council was the Prime Minister; its vice-president, the
president of the Board of Planning; and its chief secretary, the
vice-president of the Planning Board. Thus it was practically
the economic division of the Board.[5] Finally, by Imperial
Ordinance on February 19, 1938, both were amalgamated with
the Resources Investigation Council into a Planning Council
to "investigate and give counsel, when referred to by the Prime
Minister, on important matters relating to the development and
employment of national resources in all their aspects both in
peace and in time of war."[6]

Cabinet Advisory Council

Confronted with the delicate task of reconciling diametrically
opposed factions among prominent officials and citizens, Prince
Konoye decided to reinforce his Cabinet with councillors. Thus
was organized in October 1937 the Cabinet Advisory Council.
Such a body would be of extreme importance in preventing internal strife in Japan if the Government failed to settle the
present war satisfactorily. By appointing representatives of all
the factions to the council it would be possible to prevent any
single group from being accused of mistakes. Premier Konoye
also hoped that the council would serve as a training ground
for his successor. Furthermore, since this cabinet was composed largely of young men, with no party background and as
a "national cabinet" was incapable of mobilizing the entire
national power of the country, it was thought necessary to have
a supplementary institution with party representation.

As the Cabinet Council was organized "in order to participate
in the Cabinet's discussion and planning of important State
affairs concerning the China Incident," the duties of the coun-

[4] *Tokyo Gazette*, No. 1, July 1937, p. 13 *et seq.* For a resumé of the articles
providing for this board see below, Appendix I.
[5] *Tokyo Gazette*, No. 1, July 1937, p. 15.
[6] *Ibid.*, No. 11, May 1938, p. 48.

cillors were largely advisory.[7] However, they were considered important enough to be accorded court treatment similar to that afforded State Ministers. In fact, the real national policies were discussed at their semi-weekly meetings and the ministers of the various departments were thus left to deal with administrative matters. Serious national attitudes were not discussed at cabinet meetings;[8] for it was felt that "unless there is brought into being an organized body of influence equal in power to what may be expected from the possible combination of the Seiyukai and the Minseito . . . Japan will continue . . . to have Cabinets organized on the basis of compromise among the bureaucrats, the military and political parties."[9] Thus leaders of opposing factions, such as General Kazushige Ugaki and General Sadao Araki, Admiral Kiyokazu Abo and Admiral Nobumasa Suetsugu were named councillors. But in spite of the recent appointments of those advocating an aggressive attitude in China, sufficient antagonisms still existed within the political arena to cause Premier Konoye to consider resigning, first in the fall and finally at the end of 1938.[10]

The question of centralization of control was taken care of temporarily by the enactment of the Munitions Industry Mobilization Law and the establishment of the Cabinet Planning Board. The Premier, furthermore, assured himself of advice from all factions within the country through the Cabinet Advisory Council. After tightening general control over the nation,

[7] Taketora Ogata, "Behind Japan's Greater Cabinet," *Contemporary Japan,* Vol. VI, December 1937, p. 379 *et seq.*

[8] Yasushi Sekiguchi, "The Changing Status of the Cabinet in Japan," *Pacific Affairs,* Vol. XI, March 1938, p. 5.

[9] Ogata, *op. cit.,* p. 387.

[10] Other appointments to the Council included Mr. Chuji Machida, president of the Minseito Party; Mr. Yonezo Maeda, leader of the Seiyukai; Mr. Kiyoshi Akita, former speaker of the Lower House; Baron Seinosuke Goh, a business representative; Mr. Seihin Ikeda, then president of the Bank of Japan but soon to become Finance Minister; Mr. Yosuke Matsuoka, president of the South Manchurian Railway. Following the vacancies left by Generals Ugaki and Araki, Admiral Suetsugu and Mr. Ukeda upon their appointments to cabinet posts by the end of May 1938, General Iwane Matsui, former commander of the Shanghai forces, and Mr. Sonyu Otani, former Overseas Minister, were appointed as councillors. General Matsui, who had been withdrawn following the sinking of the S.S. *Panay* in December 1937, was appointed to give the council and the cabinet important advice concerning the war in China. Mr. Otani, the newly appointed president of the North China Development Company, was likewise an appropriate appointment from the point of view of establishing a unified policy in the newly occupied territories. See *Nichi Nichi,* July 21, 1938, quoted in *Japan Advertiser,* July 21, 1938.

the next step was to centralize control of actual military operations. This was done through the establishment of the Imperial Headquarters.

Under the Imperial Headquarters Ordinance it is provided that: "The highest body of the Supreme Command, to be called the Imperial Headquarters, shall be established under the supervision of the Emperor. The Chief of the Army General Staff and the Chief of the Navy General Staff shall as heads of their respective staffs assist the Emperor in the exercise of His Majesty's Supreme Command, formulating the strategic plans for achievement of the final objective and coordinating the operations of the army and navy." The Imperial Headquarters was organized on November 20, 1937, and immediately took charge of military operations on the continent. Following this, on January 11, 1938, an Imperial Conference was called to determine the definite action Japan should take regarding the conflict in China. In three of the four previous Imperial Conferences held in Japan's history, Japan had declared war against China, Russia and Germany, respectively, but this time it simply stated that henceforth it would not deal directly with the Chiang Kai-shek régime. This same attitude was reaffirmed later in the year, but Japan carefully avoided a formal declaration of war.

National Mobilization Law

The most important action of the 73rd session of the Diet in March 1938 was the passage of the National General Mobilization Bill. Fearing that the enactment of this law would mean complete loss of individual liberty even in peace-time, members of the Lower House opposed it. Passage was assured, however, when Premier Konoye promised that it was applicable only in time of extreme emergency and that the Government would appoint a majority of Diet members to the National Mobilization Council. This Council, composed of thirty Diet members and twenty Government officials, scholars and experts, was responsible for the formation of Imperial Ordinances which would make the law more effective or more applicable to changing conditions and circumstances.[11] From the time the bill was passed the question of its application, as a whole or in part, created a definite split within the Konoye Cabinet and was per-

[11] Bisson, *Foreign Policy Reports*, cited, p. 140.

haps partially responsible for its final downfall on January 3, 1939.

A brief analysis of the main parts of this law is essential since it authorized the basic steps considered necessary for the defense of the country in wartime.[12] To quote from the *Tokyo Gazette*, the law provided for "control and operation of human and material resources in such a way as to enable the State to give full scope to the efficient use of its strength for . . . national defense in time of war, including . . . incidents or affairs (external affairs) . . . which may not be called a war as a matter of policy, but one which is virtually the same as war."[13]

The objects of the National Mobilization Bill were further elaborated in a pamphlet issued by the War Department:

The Manchurian incident has brought about a great change in the condition of national defense. The situation has been enhanced by the present incident. Under the new situation the line of national defense has been shifted several hundred miles further from the national boundary and extended to Central China by way of North Manchuria and North China, a distance of more than a thousand miles. In the face of this it has become a matter of supreme importance for Japan to expand and strengthen all aspects of her national power to hold this line of defense effectively for the establishment of permanent peace in the Orient, in cooperation with Manchukuo and North and Central China. . . . For many years to come, Japan must make very serious effort in perfecting and strengthening her national defense for the realization of this ideal, and the National General Mobilization Law is intended to accomplish this end.

By the National General Mobilization Law, Japan aims to control and operate her entire personal and material resources to the fullest possible extent in order to enable her to demonstrate her national power most effectively for her national defense in time of emergency . . . to supply her army and navy with the vast amount of war materials they require in time of war, to secure smooth economic operation for the stability of national life, and at the same time to demoralize the enemy on the battlefield as well as on the economic and propaganda fronts.[14]

More specifically, this new law was made necessary by the limited character of the Munitions Industry Mobilization Law already in force. Since the re-enactment of the latter, it had been

[12] For discussions of the National Mobilization Law, see *Tokyo Gazette*, No. 11, May 1938; Kathleen Barnes, "Japanese Government Given Blank Check," *Far Eastern Survey*, Vol. VII, April 6, 1938, p. 79 *et seq.*; Bisson, *Foreign Policy Report*, p. 140 *et seq.*; Fahs, *op. cit.*, p. 50 *et seq.*

[13] "The National Mobilization Law," *Tokyo Gazette*, No. 11, May 1938, p. 1

[14] "War Department Pamphlet Explains National Mobilization Bill," *Japan Advertiser*, May 19, 1938.
et seq.

necessary to pass numerous emergency measures to supplement it, such as the Temporary Capital Adjustment Law, temporary measures on exports and imports, and a temporary shipping control law. This new mobilization law was all-inclusive and thus eliminated the need for further specific legislation. It was divided into two general parts, war-time and peace-time measures. Under the former, such vital aspects of national life as labor, materials, institutions, enterprises, capital, prices and the press might be controlled. The provisions regarding labor and other services require of all subjects a defense duty to the State which is given the right to employ or discharge workers, and regulate their wages, labor conditions and working hours. Labor disputes are prohibited or prevented by compulsory arbitration while landowner-tenant problems must be settled under provisions of the Agricultural Land Adjustment Law.[15] As explained by the War Department pamphlet:

> With the outbreak of a war, a large number of young men who are working in mines and factories will be called to the colors, and those establishments must be replenished with a greater number of operatives than before. . . . All organizations engaged in peace industries may have to curtail their activities or even suspend them altogether . . . with the result that a large number of operatives will be put out of work. The object of personnel mobilization is to adjust the demand and supply of labor to cope with the situation. . . . It calls for close co-operation between labor and capital as well as the co-operation of women.[16]

To ensure adequate supplies, Article Eight provides for the control of the production, consumption, use, movement, transfer, export and import of important goods. For this purpose the Government must make up any shortage in war materials by their purchase abroad and by stimulating the increase of their production at home, and "have them in store to provide for any possible contingency. It may be necessary for the Government to limit or prohibit the consumption of certain war materials for ordinary purposes or to encourage the people to use substitutes for them."[17] For the smooth operation of business enterprises using these materials, provision is made for direct control of vital industries, including the installation of new equipment. Industrialists operating in the same field must cooperate in the importation, purchase and sale of goods to

[15] "National Mobilization Law," *Tokyo Gazette*, No. 11, May 1938, p. 4.
[16] "War Department Pamphlet," *Japan Advertiser*, May 19, 1938.
[17] *Ibid.*

eliminate waste. In the field of capital investment, necessary regulations are provided to balance the supply and demand of capital with that of labor and materials. These include the restriction or prohibition of the formation of new companies, the control of capital increase or debenture issues, and finally the supervision of investments of banks, both national and private, to ensure the supply of capital.[18] To raise sufficient funds for the execution of war, it is necessary to establish a war-time tax system and a policy of floating public bonds to prevent financial inflation. Thus all money circulation organizations may be controlled. "It will also make efforts, in order to buy necessary raw materials, to increase export trade, to arrange financial credits, to manage foreign bonds held by Japanese, to increase the output of gold."[19] Naturally, the Government is empowered to restrict or prohibit the publication of articles on military and diplomatic affairs as well as important financial, economic and other matters, and has the power necessary to prosecute those who violate these provisions.

Beginning with Article Twenty-One, the provisions concern general peacetime measures. A national registration of people in the professions and with technical ability is provided for, and this is to be supplemented by government training of necessary technicians. Factory owners are expected not only to formulate plans for increased production in war-time and to conduct training and exercises in operation on this scale, but must hold reserve supplies of petroleum, iron and other essential materials. Profits are assured through the Government guarantee of certain rates of business profit for industries affected by the National Mobilization Law, and the National Mobilization Indemnity Commission has charge of compensations for losses incurred under the working of the Law.[20] From this brief outline of some of the aspects of the law it becomes obvious that the underlying object of the law is to secure the immediate cooperation of all nationals in every field of activity.

Another important feature, emphasized by the War Department pamphlet, is the necessity for flexible plans in its execution. This aspect also reveals the extreme breadth of the scope of the law.

[18] "National Mobilization Law," *Tokyo Gazette*, No. 11, May 1938, pp. 5-6.
[19] "War Department Pamphlet," *Japan Advertiser*, May 19, 1938.
[20] "Mobilization Law," *Tokyo Gazette*, No. 11, May 1938, p. 8.

The Government . . . must be equipped with far-reaching plans to raise efficiency promptly in production of necessary materials, their transportation and other activities to facilitate the general mobilization. The plans and preparations will differ in their scope according to the magnitude of war. . . . The Government, therefore, must be equipped with plans and preparations applicable to varying conditions.

Such regulations, which may require revisions in the future, should be fixed by Imperial ordinances for the sake of convenience instead of being made provisions of the National General Mobilization Law. . . . But the basic principles on which such regulations may be established should be embodied in the law. . . . In the application of the law, the government is to consult with the National General Mobilization Research Commission, thus preventing it from abusing its power of causing the issuance of Imperial ordinances.[21]

Thus with far-reaching provisions assured in the Law itself and provision made for its implementation by Imperial ordinance, the National General Mobilization Law made possible, with the least amount of effort, the formation of a completely totalitarian state in Japan.

In spite of the earlier promises by Government officials that the Law would not be applied during the immediate emergency, it became necessary by May 5, 1938, to invoke it in part. By decree, the articles defining the general purpose of the Law and the industries coming under its control were promulgated. The Government likewise exercised its right to expropriate private enterprises under Article 13 of the Law. National registration was ordered to ascertain the extent of the nation's resources in professional, vocational, and technical ability. The general requirements that factory owners formulate plans for war-time production and obtain reserve supplies were enforced, as was the guarantee of profits to industries affected. A supervisory commission was established consisting of Diet members and representatives from the Cabinet Planning Board. It should be pointed out, however, that most of the articles made effective at this time were those considered as peace-time measures.[22] As hostilities continued, Japan found it more and more essential to consider the application of all phases of the Law, a consideration which has in no small degree upset the smooth running of the Japanese Government, so much so, in fact, that

[21] "War Department Pamphlet," *Japan Advertiser*, May 19, 1938.

[22] *Far Eastern Survey*, Vol. VII, No. 13, June 29, 1938, p. 154 *et seq*. For articles of the Law invoked to March 1939 see below, Appendix II.

Prince Konoye was forced to reorganize his cabinet and strengthen it against both internal and external criticisms.

Changes in the Konoye Cabinet, May 1938

On May 26, exactly three weeks after the application of certain sections of the Mobilization Law, changes within the Konoye Cabinet were begun in the hope of strengthening it against the continued strain of the war. In the first place, General Kazushige Ugaki, a respected liberal and long ambitious for the premiership, but unable to form a government in January 1937, succeeded Mr. Koki Hirota as Foreign Minister.[23] According to the reactionary press, Ugaki's mission was to strengthen Japan's continental policy, to unify it in concert with the military and simultaneously to adjust the relations of the Foreign Office and the War Office.[24] Others saw as his greatest task the solution of the problem of the establishment of a synthetic Government organ to deal with the China question.[25] His failure to agree with the War Ministry on this problem in September 1938 resulted not only in his resignation but eventually in that of the whole cabinet.

Another equally important change in ministers, although it did not take place until after June 3, was the appointment of Lieutenant-General Seishiro Itagaki as War Minister to succeed General Hajime Sugiyama. General Itagaki had just returned from command of the North China forces where he had been conspicuous in the capture of Hsüchow, and he had the approval of the nationalist young officers' faction. His appointment led the way to a definite collaboration of the army with the other ministries, for his old friend, General Sadao Araki, had been appointed Minister of Education to succeed Marquis Koichi Kido. The third important cabinet change was the appointment as Finance Minister of Mr. Seihin Ikeda, former Mitsui director and governor of the Bank of Japan since February. To facilitate the inauguration of both financial and industrial control measures and to eliminate all possible friction on

[23] For a resumé of the various cabinet shifts see *Oriental Economist,* Vol. V, No. 6, June 1938, p. 341; *Japan Year Book, 1938-9,* p. 157.

[24] *Kokumin Shimbun* (reputedly nationalistic), May 29, 1938, quoted in *Japan Advertiser,* May 29, 1938.

[25] *Tokyo Asahi Shimbun,* June 9, 1938.

measures of foreign exchange and foreign trade, he was concurrently Minister of Commerce and Industry.[26]

In spite of the prevalence of military men in the Cabinet, some felt that the country would not become more militaristic and that a reformed government could bring about "harmony between armament needs and foreign relations and . . . that in the field of commerce and industry also, measures would be adopted which would prove practical and effective in coping with the actual state of affairs. Furthermore, with Itagaki and Ugaki, both from the army, in the important posts of War Minister and Minister of Foreign Affairs, respectively, the people naturally took it for granted that the much needed harmony between national defense and diplomacy could be obtained far more completely than ever before in recent years."[27] Such a strong cabinet was felt to be necessary since it was now apparent that a complete and quick victory over China, even after Hsüchow, was impossible. Any cabinet that was appointed would have to tide over the war-time situation with the maximum of cooperation.

Two other changes in the cabinet in the spring of 1938, one in personnel, the other in policy, were aimed at strengthening its position. Mr. Sonyu Otani, Overseas Minister, was appointed president of the North China Development Company early in June and his portfolio was taken over by General Ugaki, an indication of the tendency toward amalgamation of the ministries. In the field of policy, Premier Konoye emphasized the importance of the Five-Minister Conferences. This inner cabinet was composed of the Premier, and the ministers of Foreign Affairs, Finance, War and Navy. Its chief aim was to discuss measures by which warfare and politics might be interwoven. It was, above all else, a practical device for the conduct of cabinet affairs during the time of crisis.[28]

Thus, as the war continued and the necessity for the establishment of an administrative organ for the conquered territories became more imperative, Prince Konoye strengthened

[26] Marquis Kido was appointed Welfare Minister. Mr. Ikeda succeeded Mr. Okinori Kaya in the Finance Ministry and Mr. Shinji Yoshino in the Ministry of Commerce and Industry.

[27] *Oriental Economist*, June 1938, p. 341.

[28] *Tokyo Asahi Shimbun*, June 6, 1938; quoted in *Japan Advertiser*, June 6, 1938.

his cabinet both in respect to personnel and to procedure. Thus strengthened it was in a far better position to execute new legislation, such as the National Mobilization Law and the various economic and social control measures which were to affect all phases of national existence.

CHAPTER V

THE DEVELOPMENT OF ECONOMIC CONTROL

Recent political developments have necessitated the enactment of measures for national mobilization of Japan's entire economic life. As early as 1929 business and industry in Japan had felt the embarrassment of an impending depression. Machine production had been highly developed and a fundamental readjustment took the form of rationalization.[1] The first move in the direction of rationalization was made by the Hamaguchi Cabinet in June 1930 when it established a Bureau for the Rationalization of Industry and applied the "Law for Regulating Associations Manufacturing Exportable Goods in Important Industries."[2] The Bureau for Rationalization was chiefly a deliberative and advisory body, headed by the Minister of Commerce and Industry, but it could introduce necessary changes through its committees in the various industries. Results obtained by the Bureau were poor at first, because there was no coordination between the rationalization of production, distribution and consumption. Moreover, the majority of the members of the Bureau represented the capitalist class and rationalization was carried out in the interests of this class. Labor and small business were not represented and the movement did not have the support of most of the business men's associations.

Because of the lack of real success of the Bureau for Rationalization of Industry, supplementary legislation to encourage rationalization was passed in March 1931 under the "Principal Industries Control Law."[3] By this new legislation the "cartelization" and concentration of industry was greatly increased.

[1] For an admirable treatment of the whole subject of economic control, see G. C. Allen, *Japanese Industry: Its Recent Development and Present Condition.* I. P. R. Inquiry Series, International Secretariat, Institute of Pacific Relations, New York, 1939.

[2] K. Colegrove, "Japan as a Totalitarian State," *Amerasia,* March 1938, p. 12.

[3] See "Industrial Control in Japan," *Japanese Data Papers,* Vol. 14, Institute of Pacific Relations, 1933; M. Matsuo, "The Control of Industry in Japan," *Far Eastern Survey,* Vol. IV, No. 14, 1935, p. 105 *et seq.*

While the law was originally conceived with the object of encouraging rationalization, by 1935 it was considered a means for controlling industry. In certain industries, including steel, electric power, chemicals and textiles, various articles of the law provided for the inauguration of definite production control with production quotas, a system of joint purchases of material, compulsory price agreements, sales quotas and joint sales.[4]

Other legislative measures drafted and enacted during the period 1931-4 were concentrated on controlling small industries, exporting firms and special industries like iron and oil. In January 1934 a huge new organization, the Japan Iron Manufacturing Company, was formed. The State held seventy per cent of the capital of this new company, thus controlling practically all the pig iron and over half the steel production of the country. The Petroleum Industry Law of July 1934 provided for monopolistic Government control of oil.[5]

In spite of the obvious faults resulting from a rationalization rapidly but not universally applied, industrial activity increased beginning in 1932. This increase is obvious from a glance at the industrial production rate index of the *Oriental Economist*, which jumped from 96.9 for 1932 to 139.3 by 1935, and to 180.0 by 1939. It should be noted that this increase was in producers' goods, especially in the heavy and war industries, and not in consumers' goods.[6] Exports increased in value during

[4] Matsuo, "Control of Industry," p. 106 *et seq. Oriental Economist*, Vol. I, No. 3, 1934, p. 13; and Allen, *op. cit.*

[5] Matsuo, "Control of Industry," p. 107. The Commercial Association Law for the protection of small industries not covered by the Industrial Association Law of 1931 was drafted June 1932, and was in effect after October. By the end of 1933 there were 205 members. Other examples include laws passed in 1931 concerning joint sale and production quotas for export goods. See also Allen, *op. cit.*

[6] The table is as follows:

INDUSTRIAL PRODUCTION

1931–3 = 100

Year	Industrial Production	Textile Materials	Machinery
1930	93.9	89	91
1931	91.2	94	82
1932	96.9	99	95
1933	111.9	108	123
1934	126.2	119	158
1935	139.3	128	184
1936	148.8	128	210
1937	167.3	140	252
1938	173.0	124.6	295
1939	180.0	117.9	293.4
1940 (April)	171.9	110.3	286.2

the same period by over 250 per cent and were distributed over a wider area, not being concentrated mainly, as they had previously been, in the United States and Chinese markets.[7]

Other factors besides rationalization contributed to this recovery movement. For instance, the new financial policy of the Government, involving the depreciation of the yen after 1931, checked the downward trend in prices. Trading in capital goods, largely those produced by the industries most affected by rationalization, was greatly stimulated by Government expenditures on munitions, trading and shipping. This was also the period in which the industrialization movement reached maturity, and past investments began to yield profitable returns. Moreover, past trials and experiments had finally brought about an intelligent rationalization, and Japan's technical efficiency had "made a notable advance in the decade preceding the outbreak of the present war with China."[8] Obvious shortcomings in Japanese industry were being overcome, such as lack of capital, inadequate skill and experience in making and repairing machinery, poor technical training of laborers and their consequently low productivity.[9]

Some of the social implications of rationalization and control were important. For instance, rationalization was not beneficial to labor. Low wages were brought even lower by the more extensive use of women in industry, and the working day was noticeably lengthened.[10] Furthermore, there developed a rapid

---

See *Oriental Economist*, Vol. VII, No. 8, August 1940, p. 507. It should be noted that these figures differ from those given in the *Oriental Economist* prior to June 1938. At that time they said "Indices from July 1937 are our estimation based on the Indices of the Department of Commerce and Industry." In the above issue they have adjusted their old figures (based on 1928 as 100) to comply with the new index 1931-3 = 100. In quoting earlier figures care should be taken to note whether they are based on the old or new index base. See also Allen, *op. cit.*, p. 49.

[7] Allen, *The Hungry Guest*, p. 140. Of course as a result of the present conflict although figures are not yet available, it is quite conceivable that the base has again shrunk and Chinese exports have greatly increased. Likewise, increased imports and an unfavorable balance in 1937 offset much of the advantage of the improvement.

[8] For a study of "The Technical Efficiency of Japanese Industry," see Allen, *Japanese Industry*, p. 25 *et seq.*

[9] *Ibid.*; Takahashi, "Factors Affecting the Recent Industrial Development of Japan," *Problems of the Pacific, 1936*, p. 263.

[10] Yasoji Kazahaya, *Nippon Shakai Seisakushi*, Tokyo, 1937, p. 346 *et seq.* Working hours required to produce one yen worth of goods:

1929–31   Increase, .695 to .909.
1931–5   Decrease, .909 to .646.   See p. 368.

increase in labor accidents along with the increased exhaustion produced by extended hours. For instance, the rate of injuries in industrial production from 1930 to 1934 rose from 25.28 per thousand workers to 35.4 and that of fatalities from .146 to .385. Similar trends were apparent in mining disasters, industrial diseases and tuberculosis.[11]

With rationalization, therefore, came a recovery in industry stimulated both directly and indirectly by Government activity. But in the wake of this fundamental change, labor hardships were increased on the one hand and prices were raised on the other. Perfect stabilization of industry had yet to be established for a nation swinging from light to heavy industries and demanding armament expenditures equal to nearly half the budget. Consequently numerous changes in control and added restrictions were inaugurated.

The aims of both the drive for rationalization of industry begun in 1930 and of new policies which were inaugurated after 1936 were the same, namely, to augment production, to secure a favorable balance of international payments and to achieve a better adjustment of supply to the demand for materials. With these ends in view, the Department of Finance announced in August 1937 that the following additional measures were to be adopted to augment productive power: materials and funds were to be used economically and efficiently; the importation of goods which would upset the balance of international payments was to be prevented; and the Department of Commerce and Industry and the Cabinet Planning Board were to plan for the production of each class of commodity so there would be self-sufficiency in an emergency, in-

---

Annual working hours are recorded as having increased from 2,766 per person in 1933 to 2,954 hours in 1935.

A study was made of 2,189 Tokyo factories which work more than twelve hours daily. 35 per cent of these factories employed over 10 workers each and 41 per cent were machinery shops. The following facts were revealed: 66 per cent of the employees worked overtime, 46 per cent worked from 13-14 hours, and 20 per cent worked over 14 hours. See p. 369. Between 1929 and 1935 working hours were increased from 5,361,913,818 to 6,999,418,629 hours; total production increased from ¥7,759,028,000 to ¥10,836,894,000 but wages per hour decreased from ¥.14 to ¥.12. *Ibid.*, p. 366 *et seq.*

[11] *Ibid.*, p. 377 *et seq.* According to a report made by *Tokyo Asahi*, January 28, 1937, the number of tubercular patients in Japan equalled 1,200,000. The latest figure for the death rate from tuberculosis was 120,000 in one year. The Social Welfare Department of the Department of the Interior put aside an appropriation of ¥100,000 for the prevention of tuberculosis. *Ibid.*, p. 391 *et seq.*

creased production of commodities which are insufficient even in peace times, and an increase in production of commodities which would effectively bolster international payments.[12]

These were the fundamental concepts behind the Government's encouragement of certain industries, the control of prices, trade restrictions and financial regulations that were promulgated with increasing rapidity. Specific and important enactments which followed the announcement of the Department of Finance were the promulgation of a law in August 1937[13] concerning the manufacture of artificial petroleum, and the enactment in March 1938 of a statute which gave the Government power to demand cooperation from persons engaged in mining petroleum and to order them to make new borings.[14] Other enactments provided for the very strict control of all trade (amended by further legislation after a few months),[15] control of shipping, the reduction of railway rates for the transportation of special goods, including these used by the services, and the regulation of fertilizer manufactures.[16]

These measures gave the Government real control of economic life. That the earlier attempts at control (whether conscious or unconscious) fell far short of attaining these objectives is apparent from the following editorial:

It is essential that the Government shall exercise the utmost care to restrict its interference with national economic life to the absolute minimum. The Government's course just now, however, is diametrically opposed to this desirable policy. Not only are imports of such raw materials as cotton, wool, etc., placed under restriction, but the foreign exchange license system is being enforced with growing rigidity, and under the two forms of control industrialists and traders are required to go through complicated formalities at the hands of Government officials who are complete novices in commercial affairs. The result has been to undermine alarmingly the competitive powers in the world markets of Japan's harassed business men, and the effect of the faulty war-time policy on the commodity price movement has already become apparent.[17]

[12] Department of Finance, "On Economic and Financial Problems," *Tokyo Gazette*, No. 2, August 1937, p. 2.

[13] *Tokyo Gazette*, Vol. 4, October 1937, p. 47.

[14] *Ibid.*, Vol. 12, June 1938, p. 46.

[15] Miriam S. Farley, *The Problem of Japanese Trade Expansion in the Post-War Situation*, I. P. R. Inquiry Series, International Secretariat, Institute of Pacific Relations, New York, 1939.

[16] *Tokyo Gazette*, No. 11, May 1938 *et seq*; *Far Eastern Survey*, Vol. VII, No. 4, February 16, 1938, p. 44; Fahs, *op. cit.*, pp. 30-33 and 34-35.

[17] *Oriental Economist*, Vol. V, No. 1, January 1938, pp. 5-6.

The final step in establishing a thorough control of goods, including their production, sale, distribution and consumption, and in synchronizing the working of the numerous laws already promulgated, was the organization in 1938 of the "Emergency Goods Adjustment Bureau." This Bureau was to "continue in existence as long as the emergency exists."[18] Its chief function was to take over the control duties hitherto assumed by the Ministry of Commerce and Industry. Specifically, the Bureau reduced the effective demand for goods by direct restrictions on the consumption of such commodities as gold, platinum, iron, steel, copper, brass, etc.; compelled the use of substitutes such as staple fiber for cotton and wool, and alcohol for gasoline, and began a campaign for thrift and economy.[19] Simultaneously it set up a supply and demand readjustment commission for yarns, iron, rubber, leather and hides, pulp, copper, and non-ferrous metals.[20] Thus the Government, both by special legislation and the inauguration of a general mobilization law, was increasing the strength and effectiveness of its control over the various aspects of economic life.

Price Control

A common characteristic of the economy of nations at war or under other unusual strains is the rise in prices of ordinary commodities. Thus one of the most important and yet difficult tasks of those in authority is to control prices so as to prevent an unnecessarily rapid decrease in real wages or an increase in the hardships of the nation as a whole. In Japan, where rice is the chief food, rice price control attracted the attention of the Government at an early stage. Considering the social and political implications of uncontrolled rice prices, it is important to discuss briefly the history of Government action in this field.

In feudal days the sale of rice was regulated in order to alleviate the hardships resulting from famine, and during the Meiji period (1868-1912) prices were bolstered to assure the State a uniform revenue from the land tax which was paid in terms of rice. Home rice was protected by a small import duty as early as 1905, but Korean rice was not dutiable except from

[18] *Hochi Shimbun,* quoted in *Japan Advertiser,* May 15, 1938.
[19] "Japan Struggles to Control Rising Prices," *Far Eastern Survey,* Vol. VII, p. 177.
[20] Reported in *Tokyo Asahi,* May 27, 1938, quoted in *Japan Advertiser,* May 28, 1938.

1910 to 1913. Temporary control measures were inaugurated during the World War, but the first systematic measures resulted from the Rice Control Law of April 1921.[21] This gave the Government control over prices. Since 1921, the Government has imposed duties on Korean rice when necessary. Following a sharp fall in rice prices in 1930, a revised Rice Law became effective in July 1931; it introduced a license system for imports of foreign rice and provided funds for the adjustment of prices by Government purchases at a fixed rate when the prices fluctuated beyond a given norm.[22] The price paid by the Government was determined in relation to commodity prices at the time, but the system failed through the absence of control over imports from Korea and Formosa. This weakness was remedied in the next year by an amendment, and under a new law of November 1933, colonial rice shipments were placed on a monthly quota. This latest law also allowed for prices to be fixed with reference to production costs of other commodities, so that prices were kept comparatively low. In September 1937 the Government was empowered to meet any military need for rice from its own holdings and to replenish its stock when necessary by purchase at a ten per cent reduction. "Fortunately," commented one of Japan's leading papers in July 1938, "Japan is self-sufficient in food, and the price of rice remains comparatively low, while the new proposals to simplify the agencies between the farmer and the rice merchant are a prelude to a monopoly of rice."[23] However, the system of rice price control, evolved since 1921, though it played an important role, was not adequate during an extreme emergency, for after 1935 cereal prices remained ahead of the average wholesale prices, except for a period early in 1938, and by

[21] For accounts of the control of the price of rice, see: Seiichi Tobata, "Control of the Price of Rice," *Japan Data Papers*, Institute of Pacific Relations, Vol. XIV, 1933, p. 14 *et seq.*; Mitsubishi Economic Research Bureau, *Japanese Trade and Industry, Present and Future*, London, 1936, p. 176 *et seq.*

[22] Act IV provides: "The purchase or sale of rice by the Government within the empire is restricted only to such a time when the price of rice is either above the maximum or below the minimum: these maximum and minimum to be determined by the cost of production of rice, the consumer's payable price and the calculated trend price." Tobata, "Control of Rice," *Japanese Papers*, p. 33.

[23] The funds available for rice purchases had amounted to ¥1,150,000 by 1935, so effective control was quite possible. See Magohachiro Kimura, *Japan's Agrarian Problems*, Foreign Affairs Association of Japan, December 1937, p. 23, where the 1931 Law and the amendments are discussed.

November 1939 the difference between the two prices was greater than ever.[24] In fact drastic control was necessary to prevent a further increase in prices.

Equally important for a healthy national economy was the control of other commodity prices which, together with the cost of living index, had shown a rapid increase, notably since 1935. The index of retail prices had risen from 152 in 1935 to a new high level of 263 in June 1940. This increase had been accompanied by a rise in the cost of living index over the same period, from 181 to 248.[25] Furthermore wholesale prices were steadily rising for a while, contrary to trends in London and New York, and remained consistently high during the first half of 1940.[26]

[24] The wholesale price of cereals as compared with the average of all items is as follows (*Oriental Economist*, Vol. VII, No. 8, August 1940, p. 503):

	Average	Cereals
1931	100.0	100.0
1933	130.7	123.9
1935	134.0	158.2
1936	138.4	177.8
1937	169.4	181.7
1938	187.1	188.9
1939 January	190.0	217.5
March	193.8	219.8
May	196.7	225.7
July	197.1	231.2
September	206.7	253.8
November	209.6	268.3
1940 January	218.0	268.3
March	217.4	268.5
May	217.5	268.5
July	217.5	268.5

[25] The *Oriental Economist* index (*ibid.*) is as follows:

RETAIL PRICES AND COST OF LIVING (July 1914 = 100)

Year and Month	Retail Prices	Food	Housing	Clothing	Culture	Fuel and Light	All
1935	152	166	233	146	181	187	181
1936	159	173	233	151	184	183	185
1937	174	181	233	168	189	199	193
1938	191	195	234	204	199	235	207
1939	224	211	235	232	202	246	221
1940 January	247	236	236	245	204	262	236
February	251	240	236	247	204	266	239
March	254	244	236	251	208	266	242
April	259	253	236	254	209	269	247
May	263	254	236	258	210	269	248
June	263	253	236	262	210	273	248

[26] The *Oriental Economist* also gives wholesale prices, converted to U. S. dollars as follows:

	Tokyo	London	New York
1935	93.4	101.8	107.4
1936	97.6	109.3	108.1
1937	119.2	128.8	118.2
1938	129.6	106.6	103.7
1939	126.2	99.6	101.3
1940 January	124.7	111.2	105.0
March	124.3	100.0	102.9
May	124.4	93.0	102.8
July	124.4	111.5	.....

To counteract this decidedly unhealthy trend, which became increasingly marked during the Hayashi régime early in 1937, a Commodity Price Board was formed in May of that year to investigate the situation and make recommendations. There then followed a period of comparative failure in controlling prices effectively. For example, in August 1937, the anti-profiteering law, first applied in 1917 in respect to grain and eight other articles, was again put into operation[27] and soon expanded to include such articles as metals, ores, machines and tools, petroleum, rubber and pulp. The provisions were further extended in October to cover lumber, fowl, meat and eggs and the Government asked for weekly reports on important chemicals such as carbolic acid and resources like copper and crude rubber. Many of the new measures were unsuccessful largely because of the emphasis on price regulation, much of which was not legally enforceable, and a lack of proper adjustment between real demand and supply. A typical example of the futility of the ever-changing measures was that concerning cotton goods. The export and import laws restricting cotton imports and requiring use of 20-30 per cent staple fiber in textiles forced up the price of cotton. Bleached cotton reached a figure triple the ordinary price. A cotton industry commission was immediately organized to fix the maximum price of yarns and piece goods, subject to weekly revision, but it became necessary to extend the powers of the commission.[28]

The Seventy-Third Diet inaugurated direct Government control of prices early in 1938 by giving legal status to industrial organizations controlling the rubber and cotton industries. In the Diet the Emergency Goods Adjustment Bureau, the Council for Adjusting Supply and Demand and the National Local Price Commission were organized. In the textile industry a Cotton Adjustment Council and a Consumption Control Council decided the quantity to be produced, the monthly consumption

[27] This was provided under Ordinance 10 of the Ministry of Commerce and Industry, August 3, 1937, "to effect the prohibition of all profiteering that may arise . . . from cornering and withholding from the market articles for profit, . . . and the selling of goods at exorbitant prices." See *Tokyo Gazette*, No. 2, August 1937, p. 46.

[28] For a discussion of "Wartime Price Policy," see *Oriental Economist*, Vol. V, No. 6, June 1938, p. 358 *et seq.* Other inadequate regulations, besides the cotton ones referred to, concerned iron and steel construction permits (October 20), consumption of copper (November 10), consumption of gold (December 28), and consumption of platinum (January 1, 1938).

quota and the legal fixed price of cotton yarn. The last item was decided in May, and definite price fixing was extended to staple fiber, rayon, mercury, American lumber and other products, while oil and gasoline were supervised by a ticket system.

Unfortunately prices were still rising, so the Price Commission recommended that drastic measures be adopted for the enforcement of the following recommendations: (1) that the foreign-exchange rate of the current year be firmly maintained; (2) that prices of imported articles be held at levels equivalent to import costs, and export goods at levels equivalent to those in foreign consumers' markets; (3) that articles of daily necessity be held at current levels or not above those prior to July 1937.[29] Finally, control was shifted from wholesale prices and applied exclusively to retail prices; maximum food prices were ordered displayed in the shops,[30] in the hope of making the existing regulations more effective. In spite of all these regulations, prices were curbed only slowly. Some, therefore, suggested that retail prices should be more completely controlled, while Finance Minister Ikeda announced that the success in solving the question of price control would decide the success of Japan's wartime national economic plans.[31]

Thus in the field of prices, as in almost every aspect of Japan's economic life, Government control was becoming far-reaching. That measures of control often lacked the proper implementation is apparent from the slow effect the new legislation and commissions had in checking prices; retail prices for the latest date available were the highest yet, and wholesale prices were exceptionally slow in following world trends. The fact that progressive adjustments in the machinery of control were necessary was an indication that the economic structure was not in a completely healthy condition.

Electric Power Control

A type of Government regulation which is as vital to the health of the national economy as the control of commodity prices is the adequate control and satisfactory development of electric power. In this connection an inquiry office to prevent wasteful competition and to consider revision of the Electric

---

[29] *Oriental Economist*, Vol. V, No. 6, June 1938, p. 343.
[30] *Tokyo Nichi-Nichi*, June 25, 1938, quoted in *Japan Advertiser*, June 26, 1938.
[31] *Japan Times*, July 13, 1938; and *Nagoya Shimbun*, July 15, 1938.

Enterprise Act was set up in 1927, and four years later the new law was promulgated. Primarily concerned with control over the distribution and not the generation of power, it provided for the control of rates and supervision of the financial management of the companies concerned.[32] A new act in 1932 established a Central Electric Advisory Council to inquire into the possibilities of standardizing licenses and rates, but it suffered from the lack of representatives of either consumers or workers.

In accordance with the general trend toward "cartelization" during this period, the five leading electric companies formed a League of Electric Power Industry to operate for ten years with the object of "avoiding the duplication of dissemination lines and plants due to competition and improving the service efficiency in the interest of the consuming public."[33] This consolidation was desirable from the standpoint of these companies and served to eliminate wasteful competition; but it tended greatly to increase monopolistic control independent of the Government. Accordingly an Electric Power Commission was created which recommended that the Government control basic aspects of the operation of the business and that the companies concern themselves only with specific administrative problems. They recommended late in 1937 that the new power policy allow for a rapid increase in productive capacity from 5 million kilowatts to 20 million.[34] The electric power industry was one of the groups most strongly opposed to Government control. Under a threat of the Minister of War, that Parliament would be dissolved if the bill were not passed, and after the regular session of the Diet had been extended for a day, the Electric Power Law was passed on March 26, 1938. This law, which practically nationalized the power industry, authorized the government "to manage the generation and transmission of electric power, in order to lower the cost of electricity, ensure an

---

[32] For a study of early control of the electric industry see Masamichi Royama, "Electric Power Control," *Data Papers,* Institute of Pacific Relations, 1933, Vol. XIV, p. 7 *et seq.*

[33] *Ibid.,* p. 12. The five companies were Tokyo, Daido, Toho, Nippon and Ujigawa Electric Companies. They paid dividends from 4-10 per cent, controlled 22.5 per cent of the capital, 46 per cent of the units of power sold and 35.7 per cent of the industry as a whole.

[34] "National Electric Power Policy," *Tokyo Gazette,* No. 7, January 1938.

adequate supply of power and promote a wider range of its use."[35]

The seven articles included a general enabling clause to regulate both the generation and transmission of electricity and provision for the organization of the Japan Power and Transmission Company through compulsory capitalization. The primary function of the new company was to utilize undeveloped hydro-electric resources and to take over the large steam-power plants. The political parties added the stipulation that losses sustained by the control be met by the Government, and that bond holders of the old companies should be guaranteed a minimum return of 4 per cent for ten years. Thus it is apparent that the law was passed without the full support of the parties and power interests, so that friction might continue between the Government and leaders of the private companies. But the actual formation of the Japan Power and Transmission Company, with a capital of ¥730 million, meant the beginning of State control of electric power.[36]

It is comparatively easy to discover flaws in the smooth functioning of any elaborate system of national mobilization, but many of the aims of Japan's mobilization have approached realization. According to Mr. Shinji Yoshino, when Minister of Commerce and Industry, the "present China Incident also has an important subsidiary mission, that of setting up a basis for the future economic development and activity of the country."[37] This "basis for the future economic development" of Japan envisages complete Government control of industry of such a sort that national, not private, interests would profit therefrom.

It was to be expected that criticisms of these new measures should arise. However, such objections as were raised concerned themselves primarily with the methods of enforcement, and were not directed against the national mobilization movement

[35] "Electric Power Nationalized," *Far Eastern Survey*, Vol. VII, June 15, 1938, p. 140; Fahs, *op. cit.*, p. 48.

[36] For recent accounts of power control, see *ibid.*, p. 139 *et seq*; and M. Kohno, "The Nation Mobilizes," *Contemporary Japan*, June 1938, p. 85 *et seq*. Telecommunications had already been coordinated prior to the passage of the Electric Power Law on April 2, 1937, by the formation of the International Electric Communication Co. Ltd., a merger of the International Telegraph Co. and Japan Wireless Telegraph Co. Ltd. See *Tokyo Gazette*, No. 3, September 1937, p. 3 *et seq*, and June 1939, p. 15.

[37] Shinji Yoshino, "Our Planned Economy," *Contemporary Japan*, Vol. VI, No. 3, December 1937, p. 373.

as such. The Government was criticized, in a newspaper with nationalist leanings, for its reckless spending and uneconomical consumption of such important materials as metals and leather, and this was given as the real reason for the peoples' opposition to the Government-sponsored movement for economy in consumption and thrift.[38] Furthermore the Government was criticized for enlarging the duties of the police to include the right to enforce the new prices fixed by the Central Price Policy Commission. There was widespread uneasiness because some of the younger police officers made themselves unnecessarily obnoxious in carrying out their new duties.[39] In both these cases, criticism was directed against the methods of enforcement, not against the scope of the movement or the law in question.

[38] *Kokumin,* June 4, 1938.
[39] *Nichi Nichi Shimbun,* quoted in *Japan Advertiser,* June 27, 1938.

CHAPTER VI

GOVERNMENT CONTROL OF FINANCES

The function of this chapter is to complete the general picture of Government control by giving a rough outline of financial regulations.[1] It is self-evident that increased financial requirements involved an increased budget both for ordinary purposes and for the conflict in China. However, it was decided in August 1937 that appropriations should not be made for new undertakings other than those which were urgent and unavoidable in connection with the China affair. This new policy was the least that could be followed to alleviate a financial situation that had been growing steadily worse, with budget expenditures rising from ¥1,477,000,000 in 1932 to ¥2,282,000,000 for the fiscal year 1937-8, an average yearly deficit of ¥638,000,-000, and an accumulated national debt covered by continued bond issues totalling ¥10,395,000,000.[2]

These bonds had been quite readily absorbed by the Bank of Japan as well as by private banking institutions, and Japan was running on an estimated ordinary budget of over two billion yen, with a reserve fund of ¥2,081,000,000, when suddenly she was confronted with the additional expenses of the war in China. In July an initial appropriation of ten million yen was made, to be drawn from reserve funds, but this was soon supplemented by ever increasing amounts until a total of ¥2,540,000,000 was reached for 1937-8.[3] This was met by "China Incident Bond" emissions totalling ¥2,230,000,000 by April 1st.[4] In March a supplementary budget for the hostilities was presented to the

[1] See G. C. Allen, *Japanese Industry,* Chapter VI.

[2] Allen, *op. cit.,* Chapter VI, Table 24; Allen, *The Hungry Guest,* p. 153; and "Budget Estimates," *Tokyo Gazette,* No. 8, February 1938, p. 16. The percentage of the budget devoted to the armed services had increased during the same period from 28 to 46 per cent.

[3] Allen, *Japanese Industry,* Chapt. VI, Table 22; *Trans-Pacific,* Tokyo, March 10, 1938; M. S. Farley, "War and the Japanese Budget," *Far Eastern Survey,* Vol. VII, No. 8, April 30, 1938, p. 85.

[4] *Oriental Economist,* Vol. V, No. 12, December 1938, p. 788. The *Oriental Economist* budget figures for 1937 are ¥2,872,130,000.

Diet for ¥4,850,000,000 which was half as much again as the regular budget introduced at the outset of the Diet session, or an increase of 238 per cent since 1936.[5]

The important point to observe in this connection, apart from the fact that the cumulative total of war bonds actually issued by March 1939 equalled ¥6,761,000,000, is that these have been "absorbed" by the various banking institutions. However, since the outbreak of hostilities, the increased resources of the ordinary banks have not been sufficient to allow them to absorb increasingly large shares of these bonds. Thus the Treasury Deposit Bureau has taken care of 22 per cent of them, and the Bank of Japan absorbed ¥1,694 million in February 1939.[6] Obviously the strain will be in direct proportion to the length of time over which these issues must be extended, but optimism is still expressed by some who contend that "even though the budget estimates for the next fiscal year provide for enormous appropriations, they will not be sufficient to undermine Japan's economic structure to any appreciable extent."[7] In any case, the strain has already been sufficient to encourage the Government to take as much control of finance as possible. Various taxes were increased to meet rising expenditures, and the revenue for the present fiscal year was doubled, but this amounted to only one-fourth the estimated expenses. Therefore, it is possible that even more severe taxes may be imposed without too violent repercussions.[8]

[5] *Trans-Pacific,* March 10, 1938.

[6] Allen, *Japanese Industry,* Chapter VI, Table 25.

[7] *Oriental Economist,* December 1938, p. 789. The 1939-40 general account budget provides for ¥3,694 million expenditure, but increased revenue will cut down the year's loan financing from ¥1,008 million to ¥809 million. *Ibid.* p. 787. On the basis of a probable ¥400 million monthly issue for the year, the cumulative total would equal over ¥10,000 million, exclusive of an even larger regular national debt.

It is further argued by some that Japan's war-time economy is stronger than her peace-time economy and that she can easily absorb six or seven billion yen loans. Likewise the new development of heavy industry under the pressure of a defense program is considered healthy in view of the fact that heavy industries are still in their infancy. See Kamekichi Takahashi in *Chuo Koron,* March 1938, printed in *I.P.R. Notes,* July 1938, p. 22.

[8] See Allen, *Japanese Industry,* Chapt. VI; and "Seventy-third Diet Taxation Changes," *Tokyo Gazette,* No. 12, June 1938, p. 5 *et seq.* For example, the 30 per cent increased profit tax on corporations and 20 per cent on individuals applied only to the portions of the profits exceeding those of the annual average earnings for 1934-6. A 10 per cent tax became effective on dividends only when they were over 7 per cent per annum, on national banks paying over 4 per cent, and on local public bonds over 4.5%.

A financier itself, the Government profited from monopolies in tobacco, salt, and railways and was considering extending them to include sugar, beer, matches and fertilizer. It had invested by 1936 over half a billion yen in large companies like the Nippon Iron Company, in which Government control was exercised by part-ownership; and through the Government banks and the Treasury Deposit Bureau the national finances could easily be regulated.[9]

Another method adopted to alleviate the adverse financial situation was control of foreign trade, both imports and exports, so long as there remained an unfavorable balance of trade. Stated in other terms, "the problem of how to maintain the output of the munitions factories at the proper level reduces itself to that of how to increase imports."[10] Such a situation had developed from the position of Japan's foreign trade which had taken a decided turn for the worse after 1936. At that time the excess of imports for Japan proper was over ¥71 million and the figure jumped the next year to over ¥608 million.[11] This, the largest import excess since 1924, was the direct result of an increase in imports of raw materials for war purposes and the increased cost of these imports.[12]

To ease this situation, licenses were required for all foreign exchange contracts after January 1937, and by September the Foreign Trade Control Law was applied. This enabled the Government to cut import necessities to a minimum and empowered it "to restrict or prohibit the export or import of goods." War materials might be imported without permit, but severe restrictions were placed on raw cotton, wool and lumber.[13] In June 1938 the domestic consumption of cotton was

[9] M. Matsuo, "The Japanese State as Industrialist and Financier," *Far Eastern Survey*, Vol. V, May 25, 1936, p. 105 *et seq*. Also *Tokyo Gazette*, No. 7, January 1938, p. 13 *et seq*. The five companies referred to include the Nippon Iron Co., the Nippon Wireless and Telegraph Company, the South Manchurian Railway Company, the Oriental Development Company and the Manchuria Telephone and Telegraph Company.

[10] For a detailed study of Japanese trade, see M. S. Farley, *The Problem of Japanese Trade Expansion*. Also *Nichi Nichi*, June 20, 1938, quoted in *Japan Advertiser*, June 21, 1938.

[11] *Oriental Economist*, December 1938, p. 842.

[12] The total increase in imports was ¥1,019 million or 37 per cent in value and 6 per cent in volume. See Warren Hunsberger, "Japan's Position in International Payments," *Far Eastern Survey*, Vol. VII, p. 133 *et seq*.; and Farley, *Problems of Trade*, cited, Table 1, p. 72.

[13] By Imperial Ordinance dated April 15, 1937, iron imports were already exempted from duty. *Tokyo Gazette*, No. 1, July 1937, p. 32; and Bisson, *Japan in China*, p. 327.

forbidden, cotton goods for domestic consumption having already been required to include 30 per cent staple fiber since November 1937. Foreign trade immediately declined, while 700,000 to 800,000 textile workers became unemployed. Need for definite encouragement, rather than control of exports was immediately stressed. The leading industrial newspaper commented editorially:

> Japan's import restrictions since the second half of last year are telling on foreign trade. Influenced by the prohibition on imports of industrial materials and the control over domestic distribution of goods, exports are sinking rapidly. The results of foreign trade for the first quarter speak for this. Total imports fell by ¥385 million or 57.4 per cent from the corresponding period of last year. Exports declined by ¥128 million or 21.1 per cent. The aggregate dropped by 40.2 per cent.[14]

The resulting decrease in the import excess was far from encouraging, and a "link system" for foreign trade was inaugurated. Three hundred million yen of gold reserves were earmarked for shipment abroad for the purchase of goods to be used in manufactures for export.[15] Simultaneously plans were made for a stricter, single foreign trade control system, as there had been apparent weaknesses in those used heretofore. The net result was a favorable balance of trade in 1939, but when it is considered that the increase in exports was the result of trade with yen-bloc countries, the active balance is illusory. "The balance with non-yen countries, representing the actual deficit in foreign exchange, amounted to ¥624 million in 1938."[16]

Two other methods of assisting Japan's general financial status were the increase of gold production together with foreign exchange control, and the control of capital itself. In the first case, it is noteworthy that there had been an increase in domestic gold production from over ¥26 million in 1931 to ¥138 million in 1936, thanks largely to the stimulus of a gold production law of 1932. During the next year, the gold reserve was revalued on the basis of new world values, and the profits were entered in a special gold fund account. Further-

---

[14] *Chugai,* quoted in *Trans-Pacific,* April 21, 1938. For an account of the use of staple fiber see "Staple Fiber Replacing Wool and Cotton in Japan," *Far Eastern Survey,* Vol. VII, p. 23.

[15] *Ibid.,* p. 16 *et seq.*; and *Tokyo Asahi,* July 22, 1938, quoted in *Japan Times* of same date.

[16] See Farley, *op. cit.,* p. 24 *et seq.*; and *Oriental Economist,* August 1939, p. 559.

more, a new gold production law was promulgated in 1937, which authorized the Government to purchase all newly refined gold, approve and offer suggestions for plans for new refineries, and to allow the gold commission to decide its price. Machinery and tools for mining were all to be imported duty-free for a period of five years.[17]

Vast sums estimated at ¥830 million were reported to have been exported in 1937 to balance international payments, and the gold reserve was depleted to such an extent that increased gold production became imperative. On March 29, 1938, the Japan Gold Production Development Company was established to supply the necessary capital to increase gold production and operate refineries under Government supervision and with guaranteed dividends.[18] It was hoped this new company would increase production to ¥465 million in 1941; in the meantime most of the newly refined metal was to be sent abroad. Since the Department of Finance has ceased, since July 1937, to publish figures on the transfer of gold and silver, it is impossible to determine the exact amount of gold on hand. However, following the appropriation of ¥300 million for the link-system, and after a final revaluation of gold reserves, it was estimated that there remained a reserve of half a billion yen in the vaults, as of July 1938.[19]

Already the yen had been pegged at 1s2d sale value and 1s2$\frac{1}{16}$d buying value. The State also acquired the right of control over the assets held abroad by its citizens and hoped to control effectively the secret export of gold. Additional control measures became necessary at the end of 1937. They included the reduction of the maximum amount of exchange allowable for travelling expenses and for the settlement of accounts for imported goods.[20] While gold production was increased by all possible methods, a vigilant watch was kept over the funds already in the country through as strict a foreign exchange control as possible.

Finally, in a country where a few capitalists, *Zaibatsu,* control

[17] "The Gold Production Policy," *Tokyo Gazette,* No. 13, July 1938, p. 20 *et seq.*

[18] *Tokyo Gazette,* June 1938, p. 46.

[19] *New York Times,* July 19, 1938. Allen gives the figure at 501,000,000 and Farley estimates that a balance of ¥520 million existed in October 1939. See Farley, *op. cit.,* p. 74.

[20] *Contemporary Japan,* March 1938, p. 768.

such an enormous amount of the nation's wealth, the effective operation of financial control was essential.[21] Obviously this control was necessitated by the desire to have new capital enter certain specified industries, notably heavy industry, and this was implemented by the Temporary Fund Adjustment Law of September 1937. By this legislation, the Government was given the right of absolute veto over new investments. Enterprises directly related to munition materials or basic industries closely allied therewith were encouraged, at the expense of the development of consumers' goods.[22] Actually 77 per cent of the new capital approved for investment was for heavy industries, 15 per cent for the new staple fiber plants and only 7 per cent for spinning and textiles which were considered unnecessary enterprises. Such industries as agriculture and forestry were completely neglected.[23]

Confronted with an expanding budget and subsequently a larger national debt, as well as with suddenly increased expenses due to hostilities, Japan began a campaign, thus far successful, of issuing bonds to cover these disbursements. Such emergency measures were supplemented by the Government's attempts to increase its own income by new and heavier taxes both on individuals and corporations, and finally by attempts to change the trade balance. Imports, except of articles needed for war, were rigidly restricted; gold production was encouraged; and capital was directed largely into heavy industries or those needing encouragement on national grounds. Thus, in the financial sphere, as well as in the more general social and economic phases of life, Japan was subjected to drastic control in order to conserve her national strength.

[21] The banks of the three greatest *Zaibatsu* (Mitsui, Mitsubishi, and Sumitomo) account for one-fourth of the total bank deposits, while their trust companies have about 73 per cent of the trust deposits.

[22] "Investment Control in Japan Tightened," *Far Eastern Survey*, Vol. VI, p. 292.

[23] *Oriental Economist*, June 1938, p. 355.

CHAPTER VII

AGRARIAN, LABOR AND SOCIAL REFORMS

Agriculture holds an important place in the economic and social life of Japan, but in spite of the tremendous changes accompanying industrialization, it has made little real progress since feudal days. Through land taxes, a customs tax, a consumption tax and several local taxes, the Meiji Government (1868-1912) consciously aided industry at the expense of the farming class. Moreover, although the Hypothec Bank was established primarily to provide for agrarian financing, and though its regulations were revised in 1911 to facilitate the reform and improvement of agricultural enterprises, the result has been to tie up over 80 per cent of agricultural capital in land. Socially the agrarian community has been the reservoir for manpower, and the villages have had to act as asylums for children, the aged, and disabled laborers.[1] In recent years nationalist trade policies, the need for self-sufficiency in foodstuffs, and the drain on rural manpower, livestock and agricultural products resulting from the present war, have made the agrarian problem so acute that the Government has undertaken serious and long-needed reforms. Before the real significance of these reform measures can be appreciated, the special characteristics of Japanese agriculture and the problems which arose therefrom must be analyzed.

The farmers, who were "the foundation of the state" in feudal times and responsible for the income of the numerous warrior class, were overcome by tax burdens and this largely accounts for the population remaining stationary prior to 1864. Since that time, however, the population has more than doubled, and the problem of food supply for an increased population has been met by an increased output of agricultural products achieved by the cultivation of new areas and greater

[1] In 1930, 50 per cent of the gainfully employed in Japan were engaged in agriculture and fishing and in 1936 the agrarian community made up 42 per cent of the total number of households in Japan Proper. See *Japan Year Book, 1938-9*, pp. 44, 453.

productivity of each unit. Home production of foodstuffs was quite adequate before 1900, and subsequently imports from Korea and other colonies have met the increasing demand. Thus, "as the population and standard of living both increased since 1868, it is an indisputable fact that Japan proper has had no surplus population in the sense that the increased population has threatened the standard of living."[2] The problems that led to agrarian distress are the result of characteristics peculiar to Japanese agriculture as much as of any pressure from surplus population. They arise from the fact that there exists only one quarter acre of crop land for each inhabitant and practically no pasture land, and that between 1929 and 1933, while about half of the occupational workers were engaged in agriculture, the annual volume of agricultural products equalled only one-fifth the national income.[3]

Another difficulty in the agrarian situation is that the proportion of arable land to the total area of the Empire is extremely small. In 1933, only 15.6 per cent of Japan Proper and 17.4 per cent of the Empire was under cultivation. The potential increase is estimated at 1,444,000 *cho*. (a *cho* equals 2.45 acres). As a result a great portion of Japanese farming is small-scale, the average farm being about 2.61 acres.[4] Rice is admirably suited to intensive agriculture of this sort and covers 40 per cent of the total acreage.

The prevalence of tenancy was a third difficulty in the agricultural situation. The number of non-tilling absentee landowners, who purposely reside elsewhere in order to avoid taxes and the usual monetary contributions to local welfare, has been increasing. In 1936, though they made up only 20 per cent of the landowners, this group possessed 45 per cent of the total area. In terms of the agrarian population, tenants composed 27

[2] There are many studies available on the problem of population and food supply. For instance, E. F. Penrose, *Population Theories and Their Application*, Stanford University, 1934; Ryoichi Ishii, *Population Pressure in Japan*, London, 1937. See also S. Nasu, "Population and Food Supply," *Problems of the Pacific, 1927*, Chicago, 1928, pp. 339, 347. Arable land areas increased 36 per cent; rice production doubled in forty-five years from 150 million bushels to 300 million. See *Problems of the Pacific, 1927*, p. 123.

[3] Mitsubishi, *Japanese Trade*, cited, p. 151.

[4] Of the total, 34.46 per cent till is under ½ *cho*, 34.31 per cent till under 1 *cho*, 21.95 per cent till under 2 *cho*, and only 9.4 per cent till over that amount. See Akira Kazami, "Whither the Japanese Peasantry," *Contemporary Japan*, Vol. II, March 1934, p. 681; and Mitsubishi, *op. cit.*, pp. 150, 154.

per cent of the households, tenants and proprietors about 42
per cent and purely peasant proprietors about 31 per cent.[5]
Such a situation was bound to increase the distress. Moreover,
beginning early in 1929, there was a precipitous fall in agricultural prices. Prices for rice and cocoons dropped over 30 per
cent and the general price index fell in that year from 71.0
to a record low level of 42.4 in 1931. Although it had again
risen to 51.7 by 1934, the general decline had not been accompanied by a corresponding price-movement of commodities
needed most by the farmers.[6] Improvement in both these items
began by 1935, but recovery was slow compared with that ex-
perienced in the urban areas.

A more concise picture of the situation is available from a
specific study of domestic economy in agriculture at this time.
The average gross income in 1933 was ¥985 per household,
with working costs and expenses comprising 43 per cent of this
total, making an average net income of ¥565 to cover a cost
of living equal to ¥606. Actually, supplementary income derived
from home industries gave a surplus of ¥120 which did not include interest of capital invested in land, implements and
labor. The tenant farmer, who paid his rent in kind, actually
had a negligible net income. Thus, if any conclusion can be
drawn from the above survey, it is that the farmer was then,
and still is, forced to rely on industries other than agriculture
if he is to keep out of debt.[7] The problems of the landlord are
also embarrassing, for he is forced to pay 54 per cent of his income in taxes as compared with 14 per cent paid by merchants,
and land values are estimated to have shrunk 50 per cent.[8]

As a result of these distressing conditions, the rural group

[5] Mitsubishi, *op. cit.*, p. 154; and Magohachiro Kimura, *Japan's Agrarian
Problems*, Tokyo, p. 11. In 1927 there were 952,000 and in 1936 over 1,055,000
non-tilling landowners.

[6] *Ibid.*, p. 168.

[7] *Ibid.*, p. 170. In another study conducted by Professor Nasu and based on
statistics of the Ministry of Agriculture and Forestry for 1926-7, the average net
income for a part-tenant was estimated at ¥1,387 and for a full tenant at
¥987. The former realized ¥254, with 77 per cent of his income from farming;
the latter ¥59, with 71 per cent of the income derived therefrom. See Farley,
"The Tenancy Problem," *Far Eastern Survey*, Vol. VI, July 7, 1937, p. 156.

Kimura's balance-sheet of the average farm household in 1934 shows the
owner-farmer, owner-tenant and tenant earning ¥149, ¥93 and ¥79, respectively, with all groups being dependent on subsidiary or miscellaneous income
to balance their expenditures. Cf. Kimura, *Agrarian Problems*, p. 35.

[8] Farley, *op. cit.*, p. 157.

was heavily loaded with debts. In terms of individual house-holds, the farm debt increased from ¥135 in 1911 to ¥840 in 1932. On a basis of a probable increase of ¥100 per year from arrears in interest and new loans, the total liability up to 1935, the period now under discussion, would amount to more than ¥1,000 per family. This is more than the average gross yearly income of the farmer. If these estimates are correct, the indebt-edness of the entire agricultural community would reach ¥6,000 million.[9]

One of the gravest problems involved in the liquidation of this indebtedness is that of reducing interest rates to a more reasonable level; at present the average rate is 10 per cent. An-other is that the farmer is dependent on the international ex-port market, especially for silk. Between 1931 and 1934, exports of manufactured and crude agricultural products averaged ap-proximately 18 per cent by value of the total production, so that his income was quickly lowered when exports decreased in volume or value.[10]

With the increased economic activity in 1934 which followed the expansion of the munitions industry and the manufacture of articles for export, the agrarian population was confronted with an increase not only in its indebtedness but also in commodity prices. This compelled the farmer to retreat to a self-sufficient economy. In the following year rice prices were considerably higher, but they benefited the landowners and rice dealers rather than the farmers. Unfortunately, the poorest farmers, about 40 per cent of the total, were forced to sell their rice at a low price either during or before the harvest and then to buy it back for food later at the higher market price.[11] In the cocoon market, there was not a corresponding increase in earn-ings because of a marked advance in the cost of production, even

[9] Mitsubishi, *op. cit.*, p. 174 *et seq.* The magnitude of this debt has been at-tributed to high land prices as a result of the war boom, with high rents and high interest rates. *Fortune Magazine* estimates the rural debt at $1,350 (¥4,509 million based on the value of the yen at $.2936 in July 1936), a figure somewhat below that given above. See *Fortune Magazine,* September 1936, p. 28.

[10] *Ibid.,* pp. 156, 158. The following interest rates were paid on the debt in 1932: 9.8% of the debtors paid under 7% interest, 33.2% paid under 10%, 28.6% paid under 12%, 22.2% paid under 15% and 6.2% paid over 15%. See Yagi, "Farm Debt," *Kyoto Economic Journal,* Vol. XII, No. 1, p. 73.

[11] M. Hamada, "Coping with Agrarian Distress," *Contemporary Japan,* Vol. V, No. 1, 1936, p. 77 *et seq.* The market price of rice had actually risen from ¥19.94 to ¥28.00 in 1935.

though by 1937 prices had risen to nearly double their former level. Damage done by floods, as in 1934, helped to offset further the effect of rising prices of rice and silk. Even the greater demand for labor from the villages, as a result of the new developments in industry, and a noticeable rise in farm incomes were not sufficient to overcome chronic distress in rural Japan.[12] It is not surprising, therefore, to find that tenancy disputes, so far as they have been recorded, were on the increase. In fact, the deterioration in the physique of the farmer had alarmed the army chiefs so that it "is probably only a matter of time until they will be forced to admit that the present policy of overworking, underfeeding and overtaxing the mass of farmers is self-defeating." But at the same time it is noted that, "there is no sign on the horizon of the tenant farmers becoming the spearhead of a proletarian uprising."[13] Such then was the situation demanding reform.

Agrarian Reforms

How then was the Government to solve the difficulties arising from a severe depression, and at the same time liquidate the exorbitant rural debt? It realized that problems demanding immediate solution included: the rural debt, the tax system, the need for industries in the agricultural districts to absorb surplus labor, and the provision of more efficient cooperatives to improve farm management and the unfortunate tenancy system. From the partial reforms which were inaugurated, it is obvious that no systematic plan was adopted to overcome the deficiencies and that many of the problems remained unsolved.[14]

One of the earliest Government attempts to relieve distress took the form of assistance in the purchase of land. From 1922 funds were made available at low interest rates. This policy

[12] *Ibid.*; and Kimura, *Agrarian Problems*, p. 34. The total farm income as given by the Agricultural Economic Investigation Bureau for 1934 was as follows:

Year	Owner-Farmer	Owner-Tenant-Farmer	Tenant
1926	¥2,996	¥2,785	¥2,220
1929	2,551	2,265	2,044
1930	1,725	1,582	1,491
1931	790	909	867
1932	1,019	1,024	1,000
1934	1,347	1,349	1,301

[13] See Hamada, *op. cit.*, p. 81; and Galen Fisher, "The Landlord-Peasant Struggle in Japan," *Far Eastern Survey*, Vol. VI, Sept. 1, 1937, p. 201 *et seq.*

[14] Kimura, *op. cit.*, pp. 5-13; Mitsubishi, *op. cit.*, p. 181; and Fahs, *op. cit.*, p. 29 *et seq.*

affected nearly 175,000 acres of land which were either retained or acquired as a direct result of Government loans. In 1931 a revision of national taxes was undertaken, based on the rental value of the land, but this brought little relief, as the most objectionable taxes were those of a local character. New loans and relief appropriations were made the next year, but as emergency expenditures amounted to only ¥141 million, little real assistance was given to individual agricultural households.[15]

In 1925 postal life insurance funds had been made available to the extent of ¥112 million at the low interest rate of 3½ per cent, and approximately a quarter-million farmers had joined the credit associations; but neither of these measures was of particular benefit to the poorest small-scale farmers. Likewise, price control was begun in 1930, but the difficulties inherent in this made it only partially effective. Finally the special session of the Diet in the summer of 1932 passed an appropriation of ¥170,000,000 for one year for rural relief, but it should be noted that this was only one-tenth of the amount suggested by Finance Minister Takahashi. After agrarian support of the military was assured, General Araki opposed money grants to the farmers and in the fall suggested that "mutual aid among the peasants and small traders and owners of small enterprises" would be the best solution. Actually ¥238 million was expended for the years 1933-4.[16]

A more important step was the establishment of the Agricultural Economic Recovery Bureau in 1932. Plans were drawn up by municipal as well as rural committees to make appropriations to different localities to meet varying needs of agriculture. The main purpose of the Bureau was to seek an equitable division and utilization of land.[17]

In August 1933 the Farm Debt Adjustment Association Act was promulgated "to permit persons living in farm, mountain or fishing villages to form debt adjusting associations . . . with the spirit of mutual aid . . . to effect their economic re-

[15] Mitsubishi, *op. cit.*, p. 179 *et seq.*

[16] Kimura, *op. cit.*, p. 19; and T. A. Bisson, "Fascist Trends," p. 324. As compared to urban workers it is pointed out that rural gross incomes were reduced 50 per cent, management expenses 39 per cent and non-agricultural incomes increased 33 per cent. See M. S. Farley, "Japan's Unsolved Tenancy Problem," *Far Eastern Survey*, Vol. VI, July 7, 1937, p. 156.

[17] Mitsubishi, *op. cit.*, p. 180.

vival."[18] It was anticipated that by 1936 there would be 24,000 associations which would be able to adjust loans totalling between 600 million and a billion yen. Unfortunately, by March 1936 only 26 per cent of the minimum goal had been attained. This was accomplished through a reduction in the principal of loans, the cancellation of interest in arrears, the reduction of interest rates, the extension of the periods of redemption and the conversion into annual installment plans. The failure of this scheme made the reduction of rates of interest charged by the professional money-lenders seem all the more imperative.[19] Another counter-measure was the establishment in 1936 of the North Eastern Development Company, with a capital of ¥30 million, to help alleviate economic distress in the impoverished area north of Tokyo. This company received a Government subsidy for fifteen years and was empowered to issue debentures, invest in or manage fertilizer and electro-chemical industries and to exploit the maritime and mining resources of the region. Quite naturally its aims included the reclamation of land and the industrialization of the north-eastern agrarian villages, but these measures were of a local, restricted nature and could not solve any of the universal agrarian problems.

With the outbreak of hostilities in July 1937 and their continuance thereafter, the importance of agriculture, and especially of a healthy rural community, became apparent. Having failed to solve any of the basic problems by their previous methods, the authorities began to consider the problem of more thorough agrarian reform. War conditions had made the need for assistance to rural communities all the more acute. In the first place, about 46 per cent of the soldiers called to the colors were from the farm villages, and the greater portion of labor-power in commerce and industry came from the same source. Secondly, previous Government measures had been of only a palliative nature and had effected little real improvement in the living conditions of the farmer. Thirdly, the higher rice prices were benefiting only the middleman and actually increasing the farmer's hardships, as were the advanced prices

[18] Yagi, "The Problem of Farm Debt Adjustment," *Kyoto Economic Journal,* July 1937, Vol. XII, No. 1, p. 64.

[19] *Ibid.,* p. 73. The total debt for 1932 was estimated at ¥4,720 million, a figure which corresponds fairly accurately with the estimate of ¥6 billion made in 1935. See above, p. 90.

of farm implements. And lastly, the transformation of the ammonium sulphate industry into munitions plants left no means
of supplying the farmer with fertilizer.[20] The emergency measures inaugurated to solve the difficulties facing the agrarian
and fishing villages centered around three points: 1) readjustment of labor, 2) assistance for soldiers' families, and 3)
maintenance of productive power. By order of the Ministry
of Agriculture and Forestry on August 6, 1937, all labor in
the villages was to be unified and coordinated to be available
to assist neighboring villages needing more labor. The age-old
idea of a communal labor was encouraged, tools and machines
were supplied by the Ministry, and "Service Bands" were organized. These groups, under local supervision, would work
wherever needed and supply their own labor in place of work
formerly performed by horses. Parenthetically, it is interesting
to note that "the money paid . . . for requisitioned horses is
mostly deposited as the common fund of the village to be used
for purchasing new horses for the common service of the village."[21] Secondly, specific measures were soon inaugurated to
aid families deprived of their breadwinner by the war. Under
a system of soldiers' aid the families of men on active service
were paid at a maximum rate of ¥.35 per day for each member
of the family, and the Department of Agriculture and Forestry
made arrangements to have various agrarian organizations help
these families. They were to receive free advice from provincial
officials, and preference in purchasing Government-owned rice.
All school fees for children of soldiers' families were cancelled,
as were their dues in various associations. Financial assistance
was given to help settle debts or keep the family in their present
status of landowner or tenant. Special temporary grants by the
War and Navy Ministries to families of dead soldiers were
announced at ¥900 for privates and ¥1200 for corporals, but this
was far below the amount recommended by the Planning
Board.[22] Lastly, to keep up the productive power of the rural
areas, the Government concentrated on the production of eight
million pounds of "self-supplied fertilizer," the allotment of

[20] Kenichi Abe, "War Conditions and the Farmer," *Chuo Koron,* quoted in
Contemporary Japan, March 1938, p. 697 *et seq.*

[21] *Japan Year Book, 1938-9,* p. 462.

[22] Abe, "War Conditions and the Farmer," p. 694 *et seq.* The Planning Board
recommended a flat grant of ¥5000 irrespective of military rank.

about 150,000 acres of land for production of green manure, and the encouragement of the importation of ammonium sulphate. Attempts were also made to increase materials needed by the army.[23]

Convinced of the gravity of the situation, the authorities drafted a law for agrarian adjustment. This allowed for a system under which the cities, towns and villages might manage or utilize farm land on behalf of the farmers who were unable to till their own or leased land. An enabling clause facilitated the creation of new independent farmers, and to avoid tenancy disputes arising from the consolidation or disposal of land, the new organizations created were compelled to announce their plans in advance. All independent farm land thus created was subjected to approval of the authorities prior to its transfer. The livelihood of the tenant farmer was assured and stabilized by clauses which protected his lease from being affected by any transfer in ownership, and prohibited cancellation of the lease without consent of the lessee on six months' notice except in default of payments or when the landowner must cultivate the land himself. Tenancy and any other disputes which had continued to cause the authorities embarrassment could be subjected compulsorily to arbitration and the courts might order crops to be kept unchanged, hold land rentals in custody or investigate further and then resort to judicial proceedings to achieve a solution of the trouble. Lastly, commissions on farm land were established in various localities to deal with matters connected with the creation and maintenance of independent farmers, the exploitation of uncultivated land, the transfer and consolidation of farm land, tenant relationships and other problems on the basis of various local conditions.[24] Thus under the stress of war the precarious position of the farmer was realized and measures designed to cope with obvious weaknesses in the agrarian communities were finally drafted.

As the hostilities progressed, more attention was devoted to a new agricultural policy. Minister Rainei Arima announced a synthetic plan designed to link Japan's agriculture with that of Manchukuo and China, to mitigate the labor deficiency and to ease the difficulties arising for farmers and fishermen from

[23] *Japan Year Book, 1938-9,* p. 463.
[24] "Proposed Law for Agrarian Adjustment," *Tokyo Gazette,* No. 9, March 1938, p. 7 *et seq.*

restrictions on the use of gasoline and the production of implements. It was intimated that Arima would lay down a plan for securing a supply of agricultural and marine products necessary for the stabilization of the national livelihood, and might enforce a compulsory quota system for farm production, but this plan has not yet been put into operation.[25] However, new attempts have been made to readjust the rural debts. Debt-readjustment associations have been organized, with a fund of ¥500 million to be available until November 1947. This new legislation, which has been in force since December 1937, is intended to adjust irrational debts to the extent of ¥1,300 million and thus far has proved more successful than the scheme launched in 1933.[26] In half a year over 6,000 debt adjustment associations were formed and funds equal to ¥34 million supplied. These, it is assumed, were used either to moderate the terms of the debt contracts already in existence or to settle the debt temporarily in order to provide for the economic regeneration of the debtor. A new law of June 30, 1938, provided for the settlement of debts and the realization of economic regeneration on behalf of the families of killed or wounded soldiers, but this was considered a temporary settlement only.[27] Although more reforms are needed, prospects for a solution of the agrarian crisis are brighter than in the past, providing, of course, that hostilities do not put too great a strain on Japan's agrarian economy. As one writer expresses it:

Now that these defects are being gradually corrected, an all-round rejuvenation of the capitalistic régime in Japan may not prove altogether impossible. Those who are still convinced that the agrarian depression will be the basis for a total collapse of Japan's economic system will find eventually that they failed to recognize the actual state of affairs.[28]

Whether or not this statement is entirely true, the case of agricultural reform is an excellent example of the way Japan inaugurated changes and "reforms" just at a moment when collapse seemed inevitable. The question arises whether such changes in other aspects of Japanese life will be as timely and whether the necessity for them may increase in rapid progression. In

[25] *Tokyo Nichi Nichi*, June 8, 1938, quoted in *Japan Advertiser*, June 9, 1938.

[26] See Dept. of Agriculture and Forestry, "The Readjustment of Rural Debts," *Tokyo Gazette*, No. 16, October 1938, p. 23. See above p. 92.

[27] *Ibid.*, p. 24.

[28] Kimura, *op. cit.*, p. 37.

the case of agriculture it can be safely concluded that thus far reform, even though of a temporary nature, has kept pace with urgent demands for it.

Labor Problems

Equally important for industry was the solution of the vital problems raised by labor conditions. Special features of these conditions have rapidly changed and the latest statistics are difficult to obtain. Whereas in 1933, 47 per cent of the industrial workers were in textiles, legislation early in 1938 increased the decline in light industries which was already apparent a few years before. Small and medium-sized factories with less than a hundred workers included 48.7 per cent of the nation's total. In spite of a boom in munitions unemployment has continued to exist. Competition with Korean and Chinese labor has always had an adverse effect on Japanese labor, and present conditions are likely to make this problem even more severe.[29]

In contrast to this, certain factors affecting the labor situation are definitely advantageous. Japanese workers are industrious by nature, are technically skillful, are able to work long hours, are content with a low standard of living. This standard is largely determined by the income of the farmer, and as long as that remains low, there should be a supply of cheap labor.[30]

Working-hours are practically unlimited by law although the Social Bureau protected workers in munitions factories by fixing a twelve-hour maximum day with an extension to fourteen in exceptional cases.[31] In practice, although hours have obviously been increased in war industries, the average net working-day in 1935 was 9.5 hours, with two holidays a month.[32]

From the point of view of Japan's social and industrial stability, two important factors should be noted. First, in spite of low wages and long hours, the index of real wages, which reached a peak of 158.6 in 1931, declined 12 per cent, to 140, by August 1937. Since that time, total earnings for factory-workers have

[29] Mitsu Kohno, *Labour Movement in Japan*, Tokyo, 1938, p. 3 *et seq.*
[30] Mitsubishi, *op. cit.*, p. 43.
[31] E. B. Schumpeter, "Japanese Economic Policy and the Standard of Living," *Far Eastern Survey*, Vol. VII, January 19, 1938, p. 17. A previous factory law limits females and those under 16 years of age to a sixteen-hour day and prohibits work from 10 P.M. to 5 A.M. for the same groups. See Kohno, *op. cit.*, p. 6.
[32] Mitsubishi, *op. cit.*, p. 100. See below, p. 70.

increased commensurately with the rise in the cost of living. Thus, real wages are holding their own.[33] A second factor is that production costs have been reduced with increased production-efficiency, and between 1929 and 1933 there was an increase in the value of production in relation to the number of workers, their hours and wages.[34] Finally, the susceptibility of Japanese labor to educative influences allows for the possibility of new workers being rapidly trained to fill technical posts in new industries. Thus, although a temporary disruption in industry may result from a shift from light to heavy manufacturing, a potential group of new workers is always available.[35] In the field of labor, Japan's industrialists are blessed with an ample supply of cheap workers who are easily adapted to new tasks, efficient and content to live on a low standard. These factors are of prime importance in considering Japan's industrial elasticity during times of strain, and may be responsible for her present strength.

The story of labor disputes in recent years is indicative not only of a certain amount of working-class unrest, but also of the tendency of aroused nationalism to check discontent. Such disputes increased steadily until 1931, when 2,456 of them, affecting 154,528 participants, are recorded. As the wave of nationalism developed simultaneously with increased production in the metal industries, disputes decreased until 1935 when only 1,872 occurred.[36] In the next year disturbances were on the increase—20 per cent in metal and machine industries—because of attempts to reduce labor costs in smaller-scale shops manufacturing munitions, increased hardships from rationalization, and the spreading of strikes to large key industries.[37] At no time has the effect of nationalism upon labor unrest been more clearly apparent than in 1937 when disputes at first in-

[33] See Schumpeter, *op. cit.*, p. 13; and *Oriental Economist*, May 1939, pp. 338, 341. The figures given therein are as follows:

		Actual Earnings	
	Cost of Living	Male	Female
December 1937............	198	2.360	.773
April 1938............	205	2.326	.776
August 1938............	211	2.328	.792
December 1938............	212	2.560	.839

[34] Mitsubishi, *op. cit.*, p. 101, and above, p. 70.

[35] *Ibid.*, p. 44.

[36] *Tokyo Gazette*, No. 12, June 1938, p. 19.

[37] "Japanese Industrial Disputes on the Increase," *Far Eastern Survey*, Vol. VI, April 28, 1937, p. 104.

creased and then declined. During the first six months disputes had increased by approximately 50 per cent, and there was an even greater proportionate increase in the number of participants. Positive demands were made for such things as increased wages, especially by workers in heavy industries. Following the outbreak of hostilities there was only one-third the number of disputes and less than one-tenth as many workers involved. Furthermore, the complaints made by small-scale, non-union, factory-workers were quite passive—merely protesting against wage reductions or the non-payment of wages. Obviously the outbreak of hostilities and the patriotic feeling subsequently aroused had a direct bearing on this decrease, for the labor unions announced a policy of peace on the labor front after July and the rightist unions openly declared their support of Japanese expansionism.[38]

This sudden ideological conversion of labor from apparent liberalism, if not radicalism, to extreme nationalism is easier to understand when it is realized that a change in the policy of organized labor along lines "dictated by the national defense program" had long been contemplated. In September 1936 the Union of Workers in Governmental Enterprises was dissolved with a view to lessening the possibility of interrupted production in Government arsenals. As already intimated, the labor unions endorsed cooperation with the authorities after July 1937. In October the Japan Labor Union Confederation began to reorganize on a totalitarian basis, protested against foreign labor boycotts of Japanese goods and sent Bunji Suzuki to America to explain its position. Simultaneously the All Federation of Labor urged the extermination of all strikes, and subscription by labor to patriotic loan bonds. Likewise the Social Mass Party which was absorbed for a while by an ultra-nationalist party in February 1939, identified itself with the national

[38] Ryuji Sakai, "Labor Disputes in 1937," *Shakai Seisaku Jiho*, March 1938, printed in *I. P. R. Notes*, July 1938, p. 24; and *Tokyo Gazette*, June 1938, p. 21. The former records 1,455 disputes to June 30th, and 459 disputes after that date, involving 181,531 and 15,428 workers, respectively. The *Gazette* gives 1,522 and 600 disputes for the two corresponding six-month periods. The argument that hostilities reduced labor disputes is weakened when it is realized that there was a drop of 40 per cent from May to June and only 17 per cent from July to August, the month hostilities began. However, in the first half of 1939 the number of people involved in labor disputes was 81 % more than in the first half of 1938. See also Dorothy Orchard, "The Outlook in Japan," *Amerasia*, December 1939, p. 466.

unification program; then it resolved to revise its old platform which had envisaged a class struggle and decided to associate itself with nationalist activities and nationalist unity. As expressed by a member of the central executive committee:

Japanese capitalism is now standing at the point of departure from light to the heavy industries. It is due for intensification to a still higher degree, and the time has arrived for the Japanese labour movement to take a corresponding step forward. From now on, her labour unions will start on a path of healthy development and the Social Mass Party will attain its objectives.[39]

What, then, have been the most important changes both in labor conditions and in the attitude of labor toward the Government and *vice versa?* The extraordinarily rapid development in the munitions industries have led to a "limping prosperity." While skilled metal workers were in demand Government restrictions on exports were creating a million unemployed textile workers and causing a situation demanding relief pending the training and re-employment of these workers.[40] National employment agencies, though extended, reduced their efficiency by failing to register the abilities of the applicants. In December 1937 an Imperial Ordinance authorized a special investigation of actual labor conditions during the present emergency; this supplemented another investigation which had been concerned with the problem of demobilization after hostilities.[41]

One deleterious effect of rapid expansion in production and lengthened hours was the lowering of the efficiency of the workers. This has been most evident in a "go slow" system employed by some workers, which is attributed to extreme overwork.[42] Such a phenomenon having appeared, it is conceivable more workers will be taken on to allow for the adoption of shifts and more reasonable working hours. With the Minister of Welfare as head of the Central Unemployment Relief Council, two shifts were contemplated in the munitions industries. A general registration of workers, as provided in the Mobiliza-

[39] Kohno, *op. cit.,* p. 23 *et seq.*

[40] *Nichi Nichi,* July 18, 1938, quoted in *Japan Advertiser,* July 19, 1938. Various papers commented editorially on this deplorable situation, holding the Government responsible for "the stability of the nation's livelihood . . . in the face of long-term hostilities." See *Miyako* in *Japan Times,* June 27, 1938.

[41] *Tokyo Gazette,* No. 9, March 1938, p. 50.

[42] *Tokyo Asahi* in *Japan Times,* August 3, 1938.

tion Act, was authorized for November 1938.[43] Already the
Home Ministry had been conferring with the Service Ministries
over a plan to effect a smooth and sufficient supply of workers
in the war industries, and representatives were established at
such industrial centers as Osaka and Fukuoka to study this
problem. More especially in the field of labor relations it was
hoped the newly formed Federation for Service to the Nation
through Industry would mitigate all disorder. Claiming to be
a spontaneous movement arising from Government, capital
and labor, with its sponsors in favor of totalitarianism, it was
the sort of organization that was to help knit together ordinarily
opposed phases of society. Although seemingly content with
unbelievably low incomes, both the farmer and laborer were
to find that the war had stimulated the movement for their
reform. Many problems, most of them basic, still confronted
them, but for the time being any hardships which they were
forced to endure were gladly borne in the name of patriotism.
However, it is impossible to predict just how much longer
they can endure their lot without showing signs of weakening.

Social Reforms

The Government was anxious to forestall as far as possible
any unnecessary discontent among labor and agrarian groups
caused by unfavorable social conditions which resulted from
hostilities. Investigations for 1935-6 showed that, of the needy
persons eligible for relief under the provisions of the Relief
Law of 1929, only half had actually received protection.[44] Therefore, in spite of the fact that with the rise of nationalism all
political activities of the women's movement had come to a
standstill, a new law was successfully passed for the protection
of poverty-stricken mothers and children. This was the first
piece of legislation to concern itself specifically with the protection of motherhood. Its aim was to remedy conditions of distress
as well as to improve the general physical condition of mothers
and children. It provided that a mother and her children
would be entitled to State protection when there was no husband, when the husband was ill or when he had deserted his
family. Such aid as was provided was not to be given to mothers

[43] "Japan to Coordinate Labor Supply and Demand," *Far Eastern Survey*,
Vol. VII, September 1938, p. 225. For labor legislation see Fahs, *op. cit.*, p. 56.
[44] Tetsu Katayama, *Women's Movement in Japan*, Tokyo, 1938, p. 27.

with bad characters nor to those whose relatives were able to support them. The law came into force on January 1, 1938, and an annual appropriation of ¥4,730,000 was made, over half of which came from State funds, the remainder from local organizations. This was expected to relieve a total of 395,000 mothers.[45]

The Manchurian Incident of 1931 had put a stop to the more general program of social legislation in Japan, but the general national crisis created the necessity for some social reforms in addition to the protection of distressed mothers. Noteworthy in this respect is health insurance, which was first enacted in 1922, finally promulgated in 1927 and revised in 1934. Compulsory health insurance societies were formed for manufacturing, mining and transportation companies with more than five hundred employees, and voluntary societies for those with over three hundred. Workers were to receive benefits for sickness, disablement, maternity or death, with contributions being made equally by the employer and the employed. These amounted to over ¥3 million in 1934. A workers' compensation system had been previously established to cover many dangerous and unhealthy trades, including excavation industries using motive power or explosives, engineering and construction work, and transportation. Under this law approximately ¥1½ million was paid in the same year.[46] Those industries covered by the Factory Law and Mining Law with over fifty workers were required to pay retirement allowances as a result of the law dating from June 1936. Though insufficient to cope with many problems still demanding social legislation, these were steps in the right direction.

More specifically as a direct result of the present hostilities, changes were made in penal administration. Many convicts received orders for military service, and those mentally and physically fit for army service were released on probation. Others either volunteered for work in munitions industries or sent contributions to the Government.[47] Measures having the most effect, however, were those connected with military relief. In the first place, the Imperial Family donated money for the

[45] *Ibid.*, p. 29. According to another report, 950,000 persons were to be recipients of these benefits yearly.

[46] Yagoro Hirao, *Social Policy in Japan,* Tokyo, 1937, pp. 7, 17.

[47] "Penal Administration Today," *Tokyo Gazette,* No. 10, March 1938, p. 17.

funerals of those killed and large sums of money to families of front-line soldiers, and others in need. Government employees were guaranteed a continued salary and large factories were obliged to re-employ men when they were discharged from the army. The military relief law, recently revised, became effective in July 1937 and provided aid for the families of non-commissioned officers and men on active service, wounded or sick soldiers and their families, and families of non-commissioned officers and soldiers who had died from wounds or sickness. These recipients were guaranteed a daily livelihood, medical attention when ill, necessary funds for productive work, and funeral expenses.[48] Other supplementary measures included the supply of labor to help families whose men were conscripted for active service. The Ministry of Agriculture and Forestry undertook the distribution of breeding-rabbits, and the provision of necessary farm machinery to help compensate for labor losses.[49]

Of even greater importance and significance than these measures was the formation of a Ministry of Public Health and Welfare. The question of a Welfare Ministry had been under discussion for some time, but with the outbreak of hostilities in July 1937, its establishment was suspended until the authorities realized the value of an organization to control and perfect military relief, to conserve human resources for military preparations, to adjust the replacement of soldiers sent to the front and, above all, to promote the physical strength and general welfare of the nation.[50] Such a program was becoming imperative, for the physical qualities of conscripts had shown a decided

[48] Iwao Yamazaki, "Relief Measures for Soldiers' Families," *Contemporary Japan,* Vol. VI, March 1938, p. 667 *et seq.* In 1938-39 ¥15,200,000 was appropriated for relief.

[49] *Ibid.,* p. 670.

[50] *Ibid.,* p. 673; and "The Department of Welfare," *Tokyo Gazette,* No. 8, February 1938, p. 9 *et seq.* The first minister was Marquis Koichi Kido and the first meeting, as provided by Imperial Ordinance No. 26, was held on January 12, 1939. Other factors which convinced the Government of the necessity for a new ministry included:

1) The average duration of human life in Japan was about 10 years shorter than in other countries.
2) There were 7,400,000 cases of trachoma annually.
3) Children had progressed in height and weight, but there was no corresponding increase in chest measurements.
4) In 1935 Japan had 15,000 lepers.
5) Typhoid and dysentery were common and internal parasites were present in 80 per cent of the population of farm villages.

See *Japan Year Book, 1938-9,* p. 799; and Fahs, *op. cit.,* p. 56.

degeneration during the previous decade, and the general death rate was unusually high.[51]

Thus it was natural that of the six bureaus established under the new ministry, three should be devoted to health, namely, improvement of physical strength, public hygiene, including sanitation, housing inspection and food supply and, lastly, the prevention of disease. The remaining bureaus were devoted to (1) social affairs which included military relief, the protection of mothers and children and employment exchange, (2) a labor bureau and (3) an insurance board. The scope of activity of the new ministry covers the whole range of national life. Also:

In the planning and execution of immediate measures relating to the China affair, also in the plans for augmenting productive power which are making steady progress, and finally in planning for a better society, the new institution has an important role to play.[52]

The first piece of social legislation of importance to be sponsored by the new Department of Welfare was the National Health Insurance Law of July 1, 1938. This law provided for the establishment of health insurance associations in various villages and towns to render medical benefits to their members in an attempt to improve the general national health. By January 1939, six months after the promulgation of the Law, 152 associations had been formed which claimed a membership of 435,000 persons. Shortly after this a similar law was adopted to provide for the health insurance of the salaried classes.[53]

Indicative not only of the movement for control in every phase of life, but also of its effectiveness, is the increase in the functions of the police during the national crisis. In addition to their customary police duties, they are "preparing the nation for possible enemy air raids, guarding against political, economic and ideological plots and agitations and enforcing the changes made necessary in placing national industry on a wartime basis."[54] More problems confront them in connection

[51] "Health Ministry Established in Japan," *Far Eastern Survey*, Vol. VII, March 2, 1938, p. 56. Conscripts rejected per 1,000 had jumped from 250 in 1925 to between 400 and 450 in 1935.

[52] "Department of Welfare," *Tokyo Gazette*, p. 14.

[53] See Board of Insurance, "The Work of the National Health Insurance Associations," *Tokyo Gazette*, April 1939, p. 41 *et seq.*; and "Health Insurance of the Salaried Classes," *Tokyo Gazette*, May 1939, p. 20 *et seq.*

[54] "Police Activities in the Present Emergency," *Tokyo Gazette*, No. 16, October 1938, p. 14 *et seq.*

with crime-prevention, for they are faced with those offenses peculiar to wartime conditions, such as frauds and seizures, as well as increased juvenile offenses caused by mental perversions. Likewise, crimes in general, which had temporarily decreased, are increasing both in number and in degree of violence. To cope with other new situations, special economic police have been formed to enforce the economic measures of the National Mobilization Law, and higher or "ideational" police have the task of preventing and suppressing every kind of social movement which is subversive or attempts to destroy the foundations of Japanese national polity.[55]

[55] *Ibid.* p. 15.

CHAPTER VIII

THE MOBILIZATION OF OPINION

The Press

In any country where authoritarian tendencies exist, the influence of the press is important in molding the public mind to conform with the will of the central authorities. The first Japanese newspaper appeared in the form of a daily news sheet in 1870. Since then there has been a steady growth in the influence and circulation of newspapers until the ten leading dailies have a present estimated circulation of over five million.[1] Two groups dominate the newspaper world; the Asahi group controlling the *Osaka Asahi* and the *Tokyo Asahi* and the Mainichi chain, which owns and operates the *Osaka Mainichi* and the *Tokyo Nichi Nichi*. The Asahi group has expanded rapidly since its foundation in 1879 by Mr. Ryuhei Murayama, a serious-minded newspaper man. Quick to support any movement which would give it publicity and thus increase its circulation, it sponsored aviation as early as 1911, and later baseball. Its editorial policy has been more liberal than that of the Mainichi group and its liberalism has frequently brought it in conflict with the authorities and left it open to attack by nationalists. Such was the case on February 26, 1936, when the typeroom of the *Tokyo Asahi* was partially pillaged by "rebel" soldiers.[2] Although this incident seemed trivial in itself, it marked a turning-point in Japanese journalism, for thenceforth even the Asahi group supported the nationalist movement. For "with the nationalistic tendency further heightened by the outbreak of the China incident in 1937, the Asahi group of papers have made a new departure in their editorial policy

[1] For a brief account of the history and development of the press, see J. Hayasaka, *Outline of the Japanese Press*, Tokyo, 1938.

[2] Previously Dr. Sakuzo Yoshino, its editor, was assaulted and the residence of its owner, Mr. Murayama, was bombed because of a slip of the pen on the part of the former. When Mr. Hirota mentioned the name of Mr. Hiroshi Shimomura, Vice-President of the paper, as one of his cabinet members, his appointment was balked by the army. See *Ibid.*, p. 11 *et seq.*

and are now heartily cooperating in the successful execution of the various national policies which aim at placing Japan on a war footing."[3] Such criticisms as are offered are not of policy but rather of the methods by which decisions of the central authorities are implemented.

In contrast to the more moderate Asahi papers, the Mainichi chain achieved success through sensationalism, a gay format, and fresh, though often inaccurate, news—policies sponsored by its founder, Hikoichi Motoyama. Advancing editorially with the times, it has recently been one of the most ardent advocates of Japan's continental policy under the editorial leadership of Mr. Shingoro Takaishi.[4] Of the smaller papers, the Kokumin has been the most outspoken in support of the military in their control of Japanese policies and is now considered by many as their unofficial organ.

Except during periods of unusual crisis censorship has been exercised only indirectly. Acting first under provisions of the Peace Preservation Law of 1925, and later under terms of the Seditious Literature Bill of 1935, the police, under direct supervision of the Minister of Home Affairs, issued bans concerning the publication of information on certain topics. When the danger of public reaction to such news had passed, permission was granted to release it. Subjects on the banned list after January 1935 included the abolition of extra-territoriality in Manchukuo, the purchase of the Chinese Eastern Railway, the arrest of Communists, the May 15th Incident, and the murder of General Nagata.[5] Since the invocation of Article 27 of the Press Law governing the control of information regarding military secrets, press control has become complete in regard to any news which would influence the public mind along lines not sponsored by the authorities.[6] But even before this, anti-military

[3] Ibid., p. 12.

[4] Ibid., p. 13 et seq.

[5] See Fortune, September 1936, p. 99 et seq. The Seditious Literature Bill of 1935 made it illegal to publish anything with the object of disturbing army discipline, confusing the financial world or subverting the public mind. Ibid., p. 100.

[6] For instance, following the sinking of the Panay by Japanese airmen in December 1937, censorship of the press kept the public in ignorance of the real attitude of the U. S. Government and the attitude of the American people toward Japan. As in the European totalitarian states, press campaigns are now carried on to create anti-Soviet, anti-British, or anti-French sentiment, as the authorities dictate. Naturally, only the most enthusiastic reports of Japanese victories are sent home from the front in China.

criticism had been successfully silenced by self-censorship, occasional police bans and intimidation.

The influence of the press has always been limited in spite of its large circulation, the high rate of literacy among the Japanese, and a public which is omnivorous in its reading. Considered from the first as business enterprises, the papers have relied on stunts and attempted to appeal to the public rather than to cause them to think critically and freely. As already intimated, truth has often been sacrificed for the sake of a dramatic story or one appealing to the public, and this lack of principle has curtailed their influence. However, as a foreign editor in Japan has intimated, "in that it [the press] takes hints from exalted quarters about the beating of the patriotic drum and the inculcation of xenophobia, the press makes itself the servant of conservative reaction."[7]

Another most effective means of controlling public opinion is through centralized news agencies. Prior to November 1935, the two main agencies were the Shimbun Rengosha and Nippon Dempo Tsushinsha (usually known as Domei). The latter is a coordinated organization to supply and distribute both national and foreign news to 194 newspapers and to the Broadcasting Corporation of Japan, Korea and Formosa. Although claimed not to be an official news agency, it amounts to that in times of emergency.[8] Naturally much of the information transmitted by Domei comes from the information bureaus of the Foreign Office and the two service ministries, and a recent plan presented by the Cabinet Planning Board envisages the enlargement of the Cabinet Information Bureau to include agencies of the Foreign Office and Ministries of War, Navy, and Home Affairs. If such a plan is adopted, Japan will have advanced one step nearer the formation of a Ministry of Propaganda and Enlightenment.[9]

[7] A. Morgan Young, "The Press and Japanese Thought," *Pacific Affairs*, Vol. X, December 1937, p. 419.

[8] Hayasaka, *op. cit.*, p. 21 *et seq.* Similar Japanese organizations were formed in Manchuria in 1935, but the chief of these, Teikoku Tsushin, was allied with Domei after 1937, and together they cover the news from China. Domei's budget for 1938 was set at ¥6 million. The leading foreign language press in Japan Proper consists of: the *Japan Chronicle*, a British-owned daily in Kobe which has been most outspoken in its criticisms of Government policies; the *Japan Advertiser*, an American-owned daily in Tokyo; and the *Japan Times and Mail*, Japanese-owned and controlled, giving semi-official interpretations of all important national problems.

[9] *Japan Advertiser*, July 15, 1938.

Not only is control felt by the press, but every publication must be presented to the Home Office in duplicate three days prior to its publication. If the authorities decide to ban the work, its sale is prohibited and those volumes already sold are confiscated. Beginning in 1925, there has been a steady increase in the suppression of books and pamphlets considered injurious either to peace and order or to public morals. The number greatly increased following the Manchurian Incident, and in recent years the list of banned works has been made inaccessible to prevent excitement resulting from a knowledge of the existence of such works.[10] Foreign books were treated in a similar manner and many have been barred.

Education

Not only was machinery set up for the control of the press, but other means for thought control were inaugurated. For over half a century elementary education had been compulsory in Japan, so that in 1935 over 14 million students were in attendance,[11] and the opinions of all these could easily be molded by policies established by the Minister of Education. Moreover, such basic problems as the extension of the period of compulsory education from six to eight years, the perfection of educational facilities and the reorganization of teaching materials were all considered for reform.[12] Allowing the first of these problems to remain temporarily unsolved, the Minister of Education, General Sadao Araki, began to perfect educational control by launching a movement for the appointment of University officials by the Department of Education and not by the respective faculties as had been the custom in the past.[13] The final outcome of this controversy, at least as regards Tokyo Imperial University, is still in doubt since the University is extremely reluctant to give up its independence. As for teaching materials, constant changes have been made in the official textbooks until the teaching of history has come to be considered as a course in ethics and morals. Even the Minseito Party

[10] Reed, *Kokutai*, p. 98. In 1925, 25 books and 154 pamphlets were suppressed, but by 1932 the numbers had risen to 217 and 2,512, respectively.

[11] For a brief sketch of education in Japan, see, Tokuji Yamashita, *Education in Japan*, Tokyo, 1938.

[12] *Ibid.*, p. 34.

[13] *Tokyo Nichi Nichi*, July 29, 1939, quoted in *Japan Advertiser*, July 30, 1939. See also Fahs, *op. cit.*, p. 82.

willingly admitted that "national history is the source of national spirit" which alone can successfully combat dangerous thoughts,[14] so that future revisions will probably interpret past events in an even more "spiritual" manner.

Radio

Another important factor in thought control in Japan is the radio. Since the first broadcast in March 1925, the radio has been controlled by the Broadcasting Corporation of Japan which in turn is supervised by the Ministry of Communications. Thus all programs are subject to strict censorship, advertising and political speeches are prohibited and "nothing that might harm the interests of the country and its people is allowed to go on the air." By the end of 1937, licenses were issued to 25.1 per cent of all families in Japan, but innumerable listeners profited from loud-speakers placed before radio shops or purchased jointly by villagers or local units of the Young Men's Association and set up in a central locality. With listening-in almost a universal habit and news items and talks taking up over 50 per cent of the time in 1936, the importance of the role which radio plays in molding public opinion is obvious.[15]

Control of Subversive Groups

These efforts to regulate the press, education and the radio were in direct accord with the general policy of controlling "dangerous thought." This term, broadly defined, includes those thoughts and beliefs which disagree with Japan's national polity. As the central authorities become more nationalistic, the term becomes more inclusive. Thus, in 1925 the Peace Preservation Law read:

Any one who has formed a society with the object of altering or revolutionizing the national constitution (*kokutai*) or disavowing the system of private ownership, or anyone who has joined such a society with full knowledge of its objects shall be liable to imprisonment with or without hard labor for a term not exceeding ten years. Attempts to commit the above crimes are also punishable.[16]

[14] Hokuseki Imai, "Teaching 'National' History," *Contemporary Japan*, Vol. II, No. 2, p. 330 *et seq*. Although the Education Ministry decided not to revise the middle-school texts on the grounds of economy in July 1938, those already used did not lack an ample supply of ultra-nationalistic material.

[15] *Japan Year Book, 1938-9*, p. 618 *et seq*.

[16] *Ibid.*, p. 71.

Revisions of the bill in 1928 made the penalty for such subversive action either death or life imprisonment, and ruthless arrests of suspicious characters soon resulted in forcing underground whatever radical movement may have existed. Finally in 1933 came the remarkable documents of the repudiation by Manabu Sano and Sadachika Nabeyama of their former communist beliefs. Their conversion, they declared, was prompted by the thought of their duty to the Japanese nation and their realization that they had lost popular support at the time of their public hearings. The hostilities in Manchuria had made them realize that the mission of the laborers and peasants in Japan was to uphold the prestige of the Imperial Household and the nation.[17] The important point to note in this connection is that the Bureau of Thought Supervision in the Department of Education, whose object was the study of radicalism among students, and the Institute for Research into National Spiritual Culture, established in 1932, which offered special courses to reform teachers and students identified with the leftist movement, already seemed to be having effect.[18]

With the outbreak of hostilities in 1937, control of subversive groups became more intense. In October 1936 a Law Concerning the Protection and Observation of Ideational Offenders had made this possible, and less than two years later a release from the Department of Justice indicated that, "the greater part of some 60,000 radical offenders have taken the lead, with the outbreak of the Affair, in comprehending its significance and in offering themselves in atonement for what they have done in the past."[19] These conversions came about, it is maintained, because the radicals were confronted with the theoretical bankruptcy of Communism, were aware of the incompatibility of their beliefs with the ideals and traditions of the Japanese people, and were awakened to the consciousness of their being Japanese. Thus some are reported as already having joined the colors and having met death in action; others contributed to national emergency funds or sent a mission to the front to

[17] Minoru Miyagi, "Japanese Communists' Conversion," *Kaizo*, July 1933, in *Contemporary Japan*, September 1933, p. 325 *et seq.* See also "The Rise and Fall of Japanese Communism," *Contemporary Japan*, December 1933, p. 444 *et seq.*

[18] Reed, *op. cit.*, p. 92.

[19] Department of Justice, "Converted Radicals in the Current Emergency," *Tokyo Gazette*, No. 13, July 1938, p. 1.

comfort the soldiers. The agrarian converts attended special training schools and then returned home to rejuvenate their villages with the true spirit of Japan; the intellectual converts became active in the Institute for the Study of National Culture and made their contribution toward constructing a new Japanese Culture; and the working class converts were prepared to enter the heavy industries as workers.[20] After realizing that they had been mistaken in their conception of China as constituting the best illustration of the communist theory of emancipation of colonies, they saw the "Japanese army . . . playing the role of saving the Chinese people, in the face of serious difficulties, from the political evils of feudalistic militarism and from economic invasion of the Soviet Union and other Powers." Thus the report from the Department of Justice concluded that "it can be stated with conviction and triumph that there is no ideational insecurity in Japan under the present emergency."[21] Such a statement has a familiar sound, but if recent changes in platforms of the labor parties are an example of this type of conversion, it must have some basis in truth. If such a statement was issued by the Department of Justice, then it was taken at its face value and believed by the vast majority of Japanese who saw it; for the Japanese have never been taught, either through the schools or by editorial policies of the press, to analyze official pronouncements too carefully. Rather, they were taught to consider them important and significant simply because they were official.

"Spiritual Mobilization"

There are several intangible factors which influence public opinion in Japan and which may conceivably hold the country together in the future when all outward appearances indicate that she should collapse. These are such concepts as "the Japanese spirit" and "national polity" and the belief in "the Imperial Way."

In the educational framework, compulsory military service completes the lessons of patriotism, obedience and loyalty to the Throne begun in the schools. The habit of compliance with commands, which is acquired during military training in schools by all boys and indelibly ingrained during active serv-

[20] *Ibid.*, p. 2, *et seq.*
[21] *Ibid.*, p. 7.

ice, provides a powerful bulwark against the spread of ideas subversive to the Imperial Family.[22]

The reasons for a sudden rise of intense nationalism are also obvious when the situation is analyzed. Japan, it is argued, found herself left behind in the movement for seizure of lands in the Far East, but implicitly believed that freedom of trade would be recognized and that this would enable her to settle her difficult problems. Consequently, both the country and the people believed that such actions by other powers as the erection of trade barriers and the enactment of the Immigration Law of 1924 in the United States betrayed her. Thereafter many people lost their faith in the principle of dealing justly and fairly with one's neighbors.[23] It was comparatively easy, therefore, when a national crisis occurred, such as that precipitated by the hostilities in Manchuria in 1931, to find a new spiritual and philosophical basis for the nation's belief. As already indicated in discussing the position of the Emperor,[24] the indigenous cult of Shinto has taught a semi-spiritual faith in the development of Japanese history. In fact, the shift from a latent to an intensely active nationalism was so readily accomplished that some felt the Manchurian Incident developed simultaneously with the new spiritual movement in Japan whose ultimate aims were the unification of the various Asiatic races, a clarification of Japan's unique national destiny, a realization of true rule by the Emperor, and "the creation of an ideal international relationship for the co-existence and common prosperity for all nations on the basis of the ethical tenets traditional to the Orient."[25] Such ideas were obviously expressed in general terms with a view to making the possible lack of fulfillment less likely to cause criticism.

Efforts were immediately concentrated on the development of the traditional Japanese spirit. Instances of individual bravery by soldiers at the front were constantly cited, and even a Domei newspaper correspondent was extolled for the spirit in which he carried on his activities in the front lines, unarmed, yet as brave and patriotic as the troops themselves. Moreover,

[22] Colegrove, *Militarism in Japan*, p. 14.
[23] "The Open Door Policy," *Oriental Economist*, Vol. V, No. 6, June 1938, p. 354.
[24] See above p. 4 *et seq.*
[25] "The Fundamental Significance of Our Continental Policy," *Contemporary Japan*, Vol. VI, 1937, p. 493.

those at home had already enthusiastically apotheosized the three soldiers who died strapped to a bomb in Shanghai in 1932.[26] Furthermore, the Department of Education recently explained that the ideal of the Japanese people, that the whole world is one family, was transmitted from the first Emperor, Jimmu Tenno, and that the present affair was providential in affording an opportunity for all to function patriotically in their distinctive and rightful places. The individual, therefore, was not an independent entity but was dependent on the whole, was "born from the state, sustained by the state and brought up in the history and traditions of the state." Thus "individual men can exist essentially only as links . . . in the state. . . . The highest life for the Japanese subject, therefore, is to offer himself in perfect loyalty to the Throne so that he might participate in Its glorious life."[27]

The individual, having been persuaded to become a part of the State and subservient to it, was constantly exposed to such terms as "Nipponism" (*Nippon Shugi*), "National polity" (*Kokutai*) and "Imperial Way" (*Kodo*). Although a concise definition of these expressions is extremely difficult, a general discussion of their meaning may be helpful. The importance of these terms and ideas is obvious from the increased number of publications devoted to them. In 1932 two works appeared on Nipponism and National Polity; in 1935 the number had increased to seventy-six.[28] To be more specific, *kokutai* is defined by one authority as that form of state which is fixed and has been the same since ancient times though the type of government may have changed. It is the peculiar nature of the country by which such characteristics as loyalty, ancestor reverence, realism, love of nature, delicacy and skill, and purity and cleanliness are expressed. Its essence is the identification of the Imperial House with the people by loyalty, and the continuity of the Imperial line.[29]

[26] See Bruno Lasker and Agnes Roman, *Propaganda from China and Japan,* Institute of Pacific Relations, New York, 1938.

[27] "The Japanese Spirit; Its Significance in Reference to the China Affair," *Tokyo Gazette,* No. 9, March 1938, p. 1.

[28] Reed, *Kokutai,* p. 202.

[29] *Ibid.,* p. 204 *et seq.* Dr. Reed bases this discussion of *Kokutai* on a work written by Yoshio Yamada in 1933 known as *Kokutai no Hongi,* one of the basic works on the subject. Another author, Yutaka Hibino, in his *Nippon Shindo Ron* explains the fundamental spirit of the Japanese as loyalty and an unchanging reverence for the Throne. The common aspiration of the masses, he claims, is sacrifice in loyal service to the Emperor.

Partly to supplement this ideal of loyalty as well as to establish a justification, in terms of the traditional Japanese doctrine, for their continental expansion, the leaders emphasized the concept of the Imperial Way. Inspired by Mr. Yosuke Matsuoka and army leaders, *Kodo* was interpreted as a world mission whose purpose was to lead the world to peace, especially in the Far East, and peacefully to furnish each nation with her proper place. Thus, the mission of the new Japan, inspired by a traditional loyalty, was to take upon itself the task of spreading the benevolent rule of its Emperor throughout those parts of Asia which were ruled by less beneficent sovereigns or forms of government. Morals were taught, therefore, as a close-knit body of national doctrine, "highly sentimental in character, in which values have been rather hierarchized in the modern period as the nation has increased its integration."[30] The unanimity of action within Japan in connection with the enforcement of the various control measures, the approval of enormous budgets, the voluntary contributions to national defense, the constant offering of prayers at the important national shrines for the preservation of national honor, and the complacency with which the public has accepted the burden of war, are proof of the effectiveness of these teachings.

It has already been pointed out how Japanese radicals repudiated their former beliefs and were converted from belief in class struggle to belief in Japanese national destiny. It is further argued that to assure this victory, those aspects of Nipponism which are universal should be applied to areas which have been "completely occupied by the Japanese army."[31] Thus, its advocates continue, in order to establish peace in the Orient the "Spirit of Japan" must be the ideological basis of the relationship between China and Japan, and the spread of right ideas in the occupied areas is even more important than medical service and the promotion of general educational work. The whole problem is considered as a challenge to Japan to create "a culture which can really be comprehended, loved and admired by the Chinese."[32]

With the outbreak of the war, it was felt necessary to

[30] *Ibid.*, p. 218 *et seq.* For an account of the Army and *Kodo* see above, p. 43.
[31] Kiyoshi Miki, "The China Affair and Japanese Thought," *Contemporary Japan*, Vol. VI, No. 4, March 1938, p. 606.
[32] *Ibid.*

strengthen the national spirit and beliefs even further. Thus the movement for national spiritual mobilization was inaugurated in the autumn of 1937. This government-sponsored movement naturally directed its efforts toward the creation of the proper popular concept of the war through various media such as the press and public speeches. The Lower House pledged its support on September 8, 1937, of the effort to "realize national unanimity, cope with the situation with perseverance and tenacity, urge the lawless Republic of China to reflect on its attitude and establish peace in the Far East,"[33] and these ideals were constantly reiterated by leading statesmen. Prince Konoye when speaking for the movement declared that "the will to fight on the part of China must be brought to an end. We [Japan] must simultaneously proceed with the task of setting up a permanent structure of peace in the Orient in collaboration with all the constructive forces in China which will be liberated by our present action."[34]

The army added its share to the ever-increasing amount of material intended to bolster up the spirit of the nation. In a pamphlet, "Fostering the Military Spirit in the Imperial Forces," issued in 1938, it defined not only the exalted mission of the army itself, but that of all subjects. The duty of the army, this pamphlet maintained, was to serve the Emperor, the personification of Diety, in order to defend and spread abroad his "Imperial Virtue." It was to expand the majesty and glory of the Emperor and to protect the State. Naturally it was the duty of all to serve in the army if called upon to do so. Moreover, "from the viewpoint of modern defense of a country, the entire populace, whether old or young, man or woman, has the same duties of taking upon themselves the protection of the Fatherland and the proclamation of Imperial Virtue."[35] All the people were admonished to unite with "the army marching in the great, holy war [against China] in order to take part in the defense of [Japan's] unique, sublime State and the accomplishment of the Imperial task."[36]

High motives were given as reasons for the necessity of carrying on hostilities. One of the most important of these was the

[33] Bisson, *Japan in China*, p. 319. See also below, p. 120.
[34] *Tokyo Gazette*, October 1937, p. 2.
[35] War Ministry, "Pflege des Soldatengeistes," pp. 1 *et seq.*
[36] *Ibid.*, p. 6.

fear of Communism. A report from the business men of Kyoto amplified this by the statement that "the fundamental issue at stake in the conflict is whether or not China's struggling masses will be allowed to become steeped in Communism."[37] Other reports indicated that Generalissimo Chiang Kai-shek and the Nanking Government had been bent on provoking war and that Japan struck back in self-defense. China was pictured, not as a real nation or state, but as a disorganized anarchic group of rival political factions. It was maintained that the only way for China to enhance the happiness of her millions was to see that they would derive the fullest benefits from modern civilization, and to do this the most logical step was to look to Japan for guidance.[38] As the war progressed, the press played an even more important role in the formation of public opinion. In May 1938 it was felt necessary to explain the reports of the battle of Taierchwang as a deliberate attempt on the part of China to spread false statements concerning her victories in an effort to deceive the rest of the world.[39] In a further comment designed to refute Chinese claims, it was officially stated that:

The falsity of these Chinese fabrications [reports of Japanese defeats, the death of General Matsui, and anti-war movements within Japan such as mutiny among recruits] is perhaps most apparent in their ludicrous use of numbers. It is strongly suspected that the writers have merely inserted the first figures to enter their heads, regardless of reason as well as of truth. The propaganda also reveals a basic misunderstanding of Japanese psychology. The Japanese nation is not divided in the slightest degree, nor will she ever be so.[40]

Finally, it was argued, this campaign against the nefarious effects of Communism upon a helpless China was being waged, not for the good of Japan, but for the good of China herself and was championed as a holy cause. Thus, in the psychological and spiritual realm the nation was prepared to make any sacrifice or suffer any inconvenience for the glory of the Emperor and the State.

[37] Lasker and Roman, op. cit., p. 47.
[38] Ibid., p. 86.
[39] Editorial from Nichi Nichi, quoted in Japan Advertiser, May 16, 1938.
[40] "Fabricated News as Chinese Strategy," Tokyo Gazette, July 1938, pp. 26, 30. The statements in brackets are abstracts from p. 26.

CHAPTER IX

CONCLUSION

In a world full of turmoil in which new political alignments may continue to upset logical prognostications, it is difficult to predict developments in the Far East. Japan's future political and social structure will depend not only upon the outcome of the Sino-Japanese war and the unpredictable turn of events in Europe but also upon alterations in those internal conditions discussed in this study. Certain trends like the tendency toward centralized control of Japanese political, economic, financial and social life in the hands of a small group of militarists will undoubtedly continue, even after the present hostilities in China cease. Individual governments may change but the basic concepts guiding them will probably be identical.

Since July 1937 there have been various changes of Government and four premiers; Prince Fumimaro Konoye, who has held the post twice and is the present incumbent, Baron Kiichiro Hiranuma, General Nobuyuki Abe, and Admiral Mitsumasa Yonai.[1] The new governments have not yet changed the

---

[1] The resignation on July 16, 1940 of the interim cabinet of Admiral Yonai was forced when the Minister of War tendered his resignation. That the new cabinet contains no party members is of little importance for all the important parties had dissolved by August. A unique method was followed in connection with the selection of personnel. After Prince Konoye had received the acceptance of Lt. General Eiki Tojo as Minister of War, Admiral Zengo Yoshida as Minister of the Navy and Mr. Yosuke Matsuoka as Foreign Minister, this "inner cabinet" met to decide the policy of the Cabinet and to select the other ministers. The final selection was as follows:

Premier: Prince Fumimaro Konoye, former President of the House of Peers and Premier.
Minister of War: Lt. General Eiki Tojo.
Minister of Navy: Admiral Zengo Yoshida.
Foreign Minister: Mr. Yosuke Matsuoka, former President of the South Manchuria Railway Company and long an advocate of a positive foreign policy.
Minister of Finance: Mr. Isao Kawada, former chief Secretary of the Cabinet and President of the Toa (Eastern Asia) Shipping Company.
Minister of Justice: Mr. Akira Kazami, Chief Secretary of the first Konoye Cabinet.
Minister of Education: Dr. Kunihiko Hashida, President of the First Higher School of Tokyo.

policies of Japan either in relation to the war with China or to centralization of power at home. All four cabinets have promised to bring about a speedy settlement of the "China Affair," and all have strengthened, rather than opposed the trend toward centralized control.

Since the formation of the Konoye Cabinet in June 1937, such centralizing organs as the Cabinet Advisory Council, the Cabinet Planning Board and finally the Five Ministers' Conference have been perfected. Of these, the Planning Board and the Five Ministers' Conference are of particular significance. The former, as already noted, assisted the growth of totalitarianism by drafting the National Mobilization Law.[2] The Five Ministers' Conference similar to the "Inner Cabinet," consists of the Premier, the Minister of Foreign Affairs, the Minister of Finance and the Ministers of War and Navy. It became a reality on June 23, 1938. Provided, therefore, that any of the first three of these posts are held by men friendly to the military, the services will have a predominant voice in the determination of policy.[3] That the Five Ministers' Conference concerns itself with vital national questions is clear from the fact that it decided in July 1938 what attitude the Government, as well as military men in the field, should take in reference to third powers in China. Furthermore, that the military do control and will continue to control this conference is amply shown by the outcome of the dispute over the formation of the China Administration Board. While he was still Foreign Minister, liberal-minded General Kazushige Ugaki insisted that the proposed Board be only an executive organ and leave its administrative duties to the Foreign Office. The Army vigorously opposed this plan and later, forcing General Ugaki out of office

---

Minister of Agriculture and Forestry: Mr. Tadaatsu Ishiguro, Managing Director of the Central Cash office of the Farmers' Cooperative Society.

Minister of Commerce and Industry: Mr. Ichizo Kobayashi, President of the Tokyo Electric Light Co., sent in August 1940 to the Netherlands East Indies for trade negotiations.

Minister of Communications: Mr. Shozo Murata, President of the O. S. K. Shipping Lines.

Minister of Home Affairs: Mr. Eiji Yasui, Minister of Education under the first Konoye Cabinet.

Minister without Portfolio and President of the Planning Board: Mr. Naoki Hoshino.

[2] See above, p. 60.

[3] See above, p. 66.

on September 29, 1938, set up the New Board independent of the Foreign Office, with the Five Ministers as chief advisers and the Premier as president.[4]

With the centralization of control securely established in the executive arm of the Government, the power of the legislative branch waned. Little opposition to the Government's policies was noticeable. For instance, commenting on the last session of Parliament (the seventy-fourth), at its inception, the *Asahi* stated, "the government will do its best to enlighten the Diet on all matters with a view to ensuring the latter's cooperation, while all parties and factions in both Houses will support the Hiranuma Cabinet."[5] As if inspired by this comment, the Diet passed without question the regular budget for 1939-40 of ¥3,694 million, and shortly thereafter placed its seal of approval on a special war budget of over ¥5 billion. Some criticism arose in the Diet over the proposed 1940-41 budget, but the only man who really directed his remarks against the policy of the government, Mr. Takao Saito, was forced to resign. Hence the new budget of approximately ¥10 billion was easily passed and deficit bonds for approximately ¥5 billion were expected to be issued.[6]

Finally, with the inauguration of a new political organization under the leadership of Prince Konoye, more intense centralized control has become inevitable. The preparatory Committee of the new movement is composed of members from various important groups such as the cabinet, parliament, business, the nationalistic and secret societies and the press. Its personnel indicates that if a political party emerges from the movement it will be extremely nationalistic.[7]

---

[4] As reported in the *Japan Chronicle*, October 6, 1938, "The fundamental policies were to be determined by the Five Ministers and their execution was to be chiefly in the hands of the Foreign Minister, and the Ministers of War, Navy and Finance."

[5] Quoted in *Japan Chronicle*, January 19, 1939, p. 62.

[6] Of the total budget, about ¥5.5 billion was the regular budget and ¥4.5 was for the war in China. The total national debt to December 1939 amounted to ¥21.5 billion. Reformed tax laws were to increase the tax revenues by nearly ¥1 billion. See Miriam S. Farley, "No Letup in Japanese Government Spending," *Far Eastern Survey*, Vol. IX, No. 10, May 8, 1940, p. 118.

[7] It should be noted that Prince Konoye had resigned from the Presidency of the Privy Council in June 1940 to enable him to launch this new movement. It is reported that he refused to form a Cabinet unless the two branches of the armed services promised to reach a *modus vivendi* on all important matters. It is possible, therefore, that the Navy has decided upon a more aggressive policy in line with that of the Army. This is indicated by the fact that Admiral Suetsugu,

In his report to the Committee, the Premier expressed the hope that a national defense state would be created in which all the people might serve the state in their daily life. He stated that not only was there need for accord between the military command and other branches of government and for more efficiency in the parliamentary system, but, above all, a national structure should be established in which all classes of people could do their share in supporting the Imperial rule. With this as his goal, the new movement for a national party within Japan was launched by the Premier.

Thus it is safe to conclude that, politically, Japan is far more unified now than she was prior to the outbreak of the war. Just how long this unity will last in the face of protracted hostilities on the continent of Asia, and what may prove to be a pyrrhic victory, is exceedingly difficult to foretell. However, it appears that all factions in Japan's political life have now come to realize that a victory must be achieved, *at any cost,* and thus significant opposition is extremely unlikely at least until after the cessation of hostilities.

The successful regulation of economic and financial life is even more important than political control in a "totalitarian state."[8] Hence, Japan's leaders have been directing their nation toward a totalitarian control of all phases of life. In 1938 they passed the National General Mobilization Law because of danger from Soviet Russia rather than because of immediate embarrassment from the Chinese conflict. Its articles have been enforced increasingly by Imperial Ordinances. By June 1939 these included: the compulsory registration of all males between the ages of 16 and 50; the adoption of Article 11 authorizing the Department of Finance to control profits in industry and to appropriate property for war purposes if desired; the training of skilled workers; and compulsory mediation in all labor disputes. Those articles most recently promulgated provided for the regulation of employment of workers to prevent too high wages in important industries and the requisition of citizens for

---

one of the most nationalistic of all navy men, is a member of the preparatory Committee. Other significant appointments include the nationalist, Colonel Hashimoto and Mr. Kudzubu, Managing Director of the *Kokuryukai.*

[8] By means of the Mobilization Law, the army explained, "Japan aims to control and operate her entire personal and material resources to the fullest possible extent, to enable her to demonstrate her national power most effectively for her national defense in time of emergency."

work in vital ones.[9] Thus the real aim of the law, the control and operation of Japan's entire personal and material resources, is slowly becoming a reality.

Other forms of economic control increased in intensity. Since the authorities had not been successful in checking the rise in prices, further plans for strict price control were presented to the cabinet by Mr. Hatta, Minister of Commerce, in May 1939.[10] In the following month, General Itagaki, Minister of War, suggested that the prices of war materials be fixed at a definite level, that the machine-tool industry be controlled and that there be a rational distribution of raw materials. That the War Ministry felt it necessary to explain the attitude of the army on this problem indicates the importance it places on the necessity for adequate price control.[11] From this it is clear that the future will bring even more stringent price control.

With centralized control thus legally established by laws like the National General Mobilization Law, the leaders will be loath to relinquish the power they now hold in the economic sphere, and for the next few years they will doubtless claim that the situation both abroad and at home necessitates a continuance of present policies.

Quite naturally, political and economic control are not enough; they must be accompanied by financial control. The problem is to finance the war and the new war industries, or stated another way, it is to keep Japan solvent in the face of an ever-increasing national debt and diminishing foreign trade with countries outside the yen bloc. This is necessary if Japan

[9] See *Japan Weekly Chronicle*, March 2, April 4, and June 5, 1939.

[10] See above p. 75 *et seq*. In fact, it was reported in June 1939 that the bulls were buying rice in anticipation of higher prices because of lack of rain in central and southern Japan and southern Korea and delayed shipments from Formosa. This was in spite of the formation of the Japan Rice Co. Ltd. under a new rice distribution law which provided for Government monopoly in all rice markets and the prohibition of speculation. See *Japan Weekly Chronicle*, June 29, 1939; and "Production and Distribution of Rice," *Tokyo Gazette*, No. 23, May 1939, p. 4 *et seq*.

[11] See *Japan Weekly Chronicle*, May 11, June 16 and 22, 1939.

From June 1939 to June 1940 retail prices rose about 16%. More articles of the Mobilization Law were invoked on October 19, 1939, "to control prices of commodities, wages, rents, freight rates and other items to facilitate material control." Prices of commodities, costs of material services and intangibles were not to exceed those of September 18, 1939. House and land rents must not rise beyond those of August 4, 1938 and increases in salaries, wages and bonuses were prohibited. Hence wholesale prices and rents showed a notable tendency to remain constant after January 1940.

is to purchase certain essential materials abroad and if she is to prevent inflation and a lowering of the standard of living at home, factors which would eventually spell national ruin.

Even though Japan was warned as early as 1935 by the Finance Minister, Mr. Korekiyo Takahashi, against accumulating a national debt of over ¥10 billion, total war expenditures and accumulated national debt equalled ¥21.5 billion in December 1939, and the country is not yet bankrupt. Japan has accomplished what seemed impossible to Takahashi and is at present preparing to carry an even greater debt. According to the 1940-41 budget, an additional ¥4.5 billion is necessary for war expenditures.[12] By the end of the present fiscal year, Japan will be carrying the tremendous total debt of over ¥26 billion.

The question immediately arises as to how long this process can continue, especially in view of the fact that the present debt probably equals the annual national income. Japanese economists are optimistic in their belief that new loans sufficient to meet these increased expenses can be successfully floated. They point out that increased personal savings in 1938 equalled ¥3 billion. Furthermore, the income from new taxes of ¥250 million for 1939 was increased to ¥1 billion for 1940, an amount more than sufficient to meet the interest on all new bonds.[13] All this may be true but they fail to mention the fact that the absorption of bonds issued has been far from normal and that it is evident that the Bank of Japan will have to take an increasingly large share of them in the future. However, an immediate collapse does *not* seem imminent.

Less encouraging aspects of Japan's financial position are indicated by the recent trend in foreign trade. Following the enactment of the Mobilization Law in the spring of 1938, the Government concentrated its efforts on the improvement of foreign trade. Obviously alarmed by an unfavorable balance of ¥608 million during 1937, the Government first established a

[12] See Farley, "No Let-up Expected in Government Spending," *Far Eastern Survey*, Vol. IX, No. 10, May 8, 1940, p. 118.

[13] See *Japan Weekly Chronicle*, December 22, 1938 and March 30, 1939. See also Isoshi Asahi, *The Economic Strength of Japan*, Tokyo, 1939, p. 19 *et seq.* Mr. Asahi goes so far as to say that as the estimated revenue for 1938 was ¥2,300 million, Japan can afford to finance the hostilities for an indefinite period, as the present tax rate is far from being as high as during the Russo-Japanese War. At that time the rate was about 30 per cent, which would probably yield about ¥4,200 million today.

¥300 million revolving fund to facilitate purchase abroad of raw products for home manufacture into export goods. After less than a year's operation, the apparent disappearance of this amount raises doubts as to the success of the enterprise. Government policies and regulations must, however, have been partly responsible for the reversal of the trade balance for the years 1938 and 1939, when an export surplus of ¥60 and ¥658 million was achieved.[14]

In terms of foreign trade with countries outside the yen bloc, the situation is more striking. Currency figures would be superfluous if trade could be confined within this bloc on a purely barter basis, but they are essential with countries not using the yen. It is important to note that with countries demanding the use of foreign exchange the Japanese Empire had an unfavorable balance of over ¥624 million for the year 1938, and apparently an import excess of approximately the same amount for 1939. Figures for the first five months of 1940 indicate an even worse situation with a return to an unfavorable balance of ¥56 million for all foreign trade. This becomes even more significant when it is recalled that Japan's gold reserve now totals only about ¥500 million. The strain on Japanese finances will continue, therefore, just as long as Japan requires products which must be purchased abroad and as long as the trade balance with countries outside her own financial orbit is unfavorable. Restrictions on the use of imported articles and the consumption of such essential materials as gasoline are attempts at rectifying this situation. If Japan has acquired materials essential for the continuance of warfare and industry either through recent conquest or through the storage of reserve supplies, or if she will be able to obtain them in the immediate future through barter, then the importance of an exhausted gold reserve becomes less. In other words, unless Japan is able to improve her trade balance sufficiently so that she can make her gold reserve and her estimated annual gold production of ¥250 million cover the purchase of the bare necessities from abroad, her position will be untenable and drastic action may follow.[15]

The trend toward centralization of power has continued dur-

---

[14] See *Oriental Economist*, August 1940, p. 510.

[15] This may take the form of further expansion to the south, closer ties with the Axis Powers, and a friendly attitude toward the Soviet Union. In any event these will be conditioned by developments in the European War.

ing the past few months. In the political field, in spite of cabinet changes, there has been no change of policy. The enactment of further articles of the Mobilization Law and new measures for price control have extended Government supervision over Japan's economic life. The national debt has increased and foreign trade continues to be a strain on Japan's depleted gold reserves. Government manipulation of finances becomes inevitable if a panic is to be avoided.

With the increase in industrial production, prosperity has come to the skilled worker, but it is a "limping prosperity" for the textile worker whose mill has been closed as a result of trade restrictions. More recently a shortage of hydro-electric power has produced a curtailment in some industries, especially those of cotton cloth and fertilizer. For the farmer the rural debt of approximately ¥1,000 per family still remains a serious problem, and in addition he must rationalize his production in spite of livestock requisitions and the depletion of man-power. Deficiency in farm labor is a real problem as indicated in recent pronouncements of the Ministry of Agriculture on the problem of labor power in the rural communities.[16] The Government is regulating the business and profits of the large industrialist with increasing vigor and new restrictions conflict with the personal liberty of the ordinary citizen. The soldier has been intoxicated with the success of brute force and is just now confronted with the inglorious task either of patrol duty or garrison service in a land where everyone is hostile to him, and where guerrilla activity threatens his safety. Thus in all walks of life the situation is full of potential dissatisfaction, unrest and danger, but veneration for the Throne and an inherent com-placency on the part of all subjects have a tremendous stabiliz-ing effect. The idea of regimentation has been instilled in every-one since childhood. The Department of Education repeated only that which all believed when it declared recently that:

> The individual is not an entity but dependent on the whole, born from the state and sustained by it. The highest life for the Japanese subject, therefore, is to offer himself in perfect loyalty to the throne.

To assure the continuance of proper support and the coop-eration of the people as a whole and to stimulate the move-

[16] See Department of Agriculture, "The Problem of Labor Power in Rural Communities," *Tokyo Gazette*, Vol. III, No. 1, July 1939.

ment for "spiritual mobilization," the National Spiritual Mobilization Commission was established in March 1939. Under the supervision of the prime minister, it had a chairman chosen from among the ministers of State and a membership of sixty.[17] Its first task was the formation of a program which would inform the entire nation that "the destiny of the Empire hangs exclusively on the manner in which the present Affair is settled."[18]

Such an objective presupposes an eventual military victory for Japan. The longer the conflict continues the more embarrassing it will be for her unless present occupied areas are pacified sufficiently to permit the exploitation of resources. Without this result, it seems inevitable that more centralization of control will follow and that the people will be asked to make even greater sacrifices. Regardless of the inherent dangers in so doing, Japan believes at present that by continuing the use of force against any and all opposition in China, she will be able successfully to direct the destiny of the Far East. Any real threat to or frustration of Japan's present plans is likely to lead to even more extensive hostilities, possibly against a third power. Unfortunately, any of these alternatives would still leave the great problems confronting Japan at home unsolved: the steady trend toward inflation as indicated by rising prices, the terrific national debt, the unfavorable balance of trade and lack of self-sufficiency in many vital products, the debt and dearth of manpower among the peasants, and the danger of a lapse in the war psychosis. In fact, it is hard to see how continued hostilities will have any effect other than aggravation of these conditions.

In conclusion, it should be noted that in spite of Japan's embarkation upon a program which has temporarily weakened her financial and economic structure, her leaders are resolved to see it through. Thus articulate criticisms at home of either present or future policies will be met with ruthless suppression; additional external pressure on either Japan's economic or military front will be met with the same spirit and is likely to lead the country into more aggressive action. Those now in control may be unable to hold their present position permanently but they have so permeated the present structure of

[17] See Bureau of Information, "Further Enlightenment on the Significance of the Current Emergency," *Tokyo Gazette*, Vol. III, July 1939, p. 32 *et seq*.
[18] *Ibid.*, p. 32.

government and have so effectively perfected control measures in all phases of life that their displacement would involve the overthrow of the whole political structure. Such a contingency is not indicated by a study of conditions in Japan as they now exist but a continuation of present policies may so intensify conditions at home and abroad that the burden will become unbearable.

APPENDIX I

FUNCTIONS OF THE BOARD OF PLANNING AS PROVIDED BY IMPERIAL ORDINANCE, MAY 14, 1937

Article 1: To make recommendations, acting on the instruction of the Prime Minister, with pertinent observations, both in regard to important national policies and to their coordination and adjustment.

Article 2: To investigate the important policies proposed to the Cabinet by its Ministers, and to make recommendations based on due observation of them. Policies proposed by different Departments are referred to the Board, which is to study them in the light of their importance, and investigate them from the point of view of the synthesized unity of all national policies.

Article 3: To investigate important policies, and to study the means of coordinating and adjusting them.

Article 4: To make recommendations concerning control over budget estimates on proposed policies.

Article 5: To have authority to call for explanations or explanatory data in case such are deemed necessary for carrying out the functions outlined above.

Quoted from *Tokyo Gazette*, July 1937, pp. 14-15.

APPENDIX II

INVOCATION OF THE NATIONAL GENERAL MOBILIZATION PLAN

Imperial Ordinances Already Issued or Ready for Promulgation	Under Provisions of	Date Referred to the Council
Ordinance Restricting Employment of School Graduates (Imperial Ordinance No. 599 of August 24, 1938)	Article 6	August 10, 1938
Ordinance Controlling Factories and Workshops (Imperial Ordinance No. 318 of May 5, 1938)	" 13	"
Ordinance Concerning Declaration of Vocational Abilities of Persons Engaging in Medical Services (Imperial Ordinance No. 600 of August 24, 1938)	" 21	"
Ordinance Concerning Declaration of Vocational Abilities of the People (Imperial Ordinance No. 5 of January 7, 1939)	" 21	December 5, 1938
Regulations Governing the National General Mobilization Compensation Commission (Imperial Ordinance No. 474 of July 2, 1938)	" 29	"
Ordinance Concerning Organization of the National General Mobilization Council (Imperial Ordinance No. 319 of May 4, 1938)	" 50	"
A Summary Draft of an Imperial Ordinance restricting employment of operatives	" 6	"
A Summary Draft of an Imperial Ordinance pertaining to the control of wages	" 6	December 22, 1938
A Summary Draft of an Imperial Ordinance restricting working hours in factories	" 6	"
A Summary Draft of an Imperial Ordinance pertaining to use and expropriation of goods within the purview of the General Mobilization Law	" 10	"
A Summary Draft of an Imperial Ordinance restricting corporation dividends	" 11	"
A Summary Draft of an Imperial Ordinance pertaining to use and expropriation of factories and workshops	" 13	"
A Summary Draft of an Imperial Ordinance pertaining to management, use or expropriation of land, houses or other constructions	" 13	"

Imperial Ordinances Already Issued or Ready for Promulgation	Under Provisions of	Date Referred to the Council
A Summary Draft of an Imperial Ordinance pertaining to establishment of new industrial equipment, expansion or improvement of existing equipment............	” 16	October 31, 1938
A Summary Draft of an Imperial Ordinance concerning the declaration of vocational abilities of mariners...................	Article 21	December 5, 1938
A Summary Draft of an Imperial Ordinance concerning the declaration of professional abilities of veterinary surgeons...........	” 21	December 22, 1938
A Summary Draft of an Imperial Ordinance pertaining to training of technicians at schools and training institutions.........	” 22	October 31, 1938
A Summary Draft of an Imperial Ordinance pertaining to training of skilled labor in factories and workshops...............	” 22	”
A Summary Draft of an Imperial Ordinance pertaining to training of navigators.......	” 22	December 5, 1938
A Summary Draft of an Imperial Ordinance pertaining to formulation and rehearsal in operation of plans concerning general mobilization which shall be assigned to proprietors of industrial enterprises.........	” 24	December 22, 1938
A Summary Draft of an Imperial Ordinance pertaining to experiments and research...	” 25	”

Tokyo Gazette, March 1939, pp. 20–1.

BIBLIOGRAPHICAL NOTE

Any study such as that of the most recent political and social developments of Japan necessarily presents a difficult bibliographical problem. In the first place, much material is obtainable only in periodical form whether it be the daily press or less frequently published journals. Furthermore, it is extremely difficult to verify some reports which must be taken at their face value until subsequent events or a longer historical perspective prove them to be false. The purpose of the following list, therefore, is not to give an exhaustive one but merely to indicate further readings that might profitably be pursued. Fortunately there is an ample supply of further bibliographical material available. The chief monographs on various aspects of Japanese civilization, together with critical comments on them will be found in Hugh Borton, Serge Elisseef and Edwin O. Reischauer, *A List of Selected Works on Japan,* Washington, 1940. Contemporary books and articles on Eastern Asia are listed in Earl H. Pritchard, *Bulletin of Far Eastern Bibliography,* Washington, 1936, while a complete list of books published each year in Japan, topically arranged, appears in Tokyo Shoseki Kumiai, editors, *Shuppan Nen kan.*

Since the general problem of the availability and value of reports of government documents, the daily press and journals both in Japanese and English have been adequately treated by Charles B. Fahs in his *Government in Japan* (p. 90 *et seq.*), other points will be emphasized below. Material which is of special importance for Japan's political and social development includes the *Far Eastern Survey,* the fortnightly research service of the American Council of the Institute of Pacific Relations, *Pacific Affairs,* a quarterly journal published by the International Secretariat of the Institute, the *Reports of the Foreign Policy Association,* the *Monthly Circular* of economic and financial information published by the Mitsubishi Economic Research Bureau in Tokyo and *Fortune Magazine* for September 1936 which was a special issue on Japan. For reference purposes *The Japan Year Book,* the annual publication of the Foreign Affairs Association of Japan and the *Japan-Manchoukuo Year Book,* a cyclopedia of general information and statistics on Japan and Manchukuo since 1933, are valuable. One further point should be noted. After the recent sale of the American-owned *Japan Advertiser* to the Japanese-owned *Japan Times and Mail,* the *Japan*

131

Chronicle (Kobe) remains the only English daily owned by foreigners in Japan. Hence the significance of news reports and interpretations this paper and its weekly edition give are of extreme importance.

Aside from the other monographs in the Inquiry Series mentioned in the preface, two other groups of studies which treat of the various problems facing Japan both internally and externally should be mentioned. Published as the proceedings of the biennial conferences of the Institute of Pacific Relations, the *Problems of the Pacific 1927-1939* offer valuable comments and documentation of subjects such as the economic development of the Far East, the position of Japan in Manchuria prior to 1929, the economic and cultural relations in the Pacific, economic conflict and control and the results thereof, and finally the Far Eastern War and its meaning for the world. As supplementary documentation for these conferences, the *Data Papers* compiled by the Japanese Council of the Institute are extremely valuable. The second series of studies, though much less pretentious and lacking specific references in most cases, yet presented in a convenient form, are the pamphlets published by the Foreign Affairs Association of Japan on such subjects as the press, social policy, women, politics and political parties and agrarian problems. In using these, however, the reader should be aware of the fact that controversial material will either be omitted or presented from the Japanese viewpoint. In fact, as general control of the press continues, it will be increasingly difficult to obtain full information from Japan.

GENERAL WORKS

ALLEN, G. C. *Japan the Hungry Guest*. London. 1938.

———. *Japanese Industry: Its Recent Development and Present Condition*. I. P. R. Inquiry Series. New York. 1939.

ANGUS, HENRY F. *The Problem of Peaceful Change in the Pacific Area*. New York. 1937.

ASAHI, ISOSHI. *The Economic Strength of Japan*. Tokyo. 1939.

ASAHI ECONOMIC CHRONICLE (editor). *Senji Taiseika no Nihon Keizai* (Japanese Economies during Wartime). Tokyo. 1938.

ASAHI SHIMBUN. *Gendai Seiji no Doko*. Movements of Present-day Government. Tokyo. 1938.

BISSON, T. A. *American Far Eastern Policy 1931-1940*. I. P. R. Inquiry Series. New York. 1940.

———. *Japan in China*. New York. 1938.

BORTON, HUGH, ELISSEEF, SERGE and REISCHAUER, EDWIN O. *A List of Selected Works on Japan*. Washington. 1940.

CAUSTON, E. E. N. *Militarism and Foreign Policy in Japan.* London. 1936.

CHAMBERLIN, WILLIAM H. *Japan over Asia.* Boston. 1937.

COLEGROVE, KENNETH. *Militarism in Japan.* Boston. 1936.

CONDLIFFE, J. B. (editor). See: *Problems of the Pacific 1927* and *1929.*

FAHS, CHARLES B. *Government in Japan.* I. P. R. Inquiry Series. New York. 1940.

FARLEY, MIRIAM S. *The Problem of Japanese Trade Expansion in the Post-War Situation.* I. P. R. Inquiry Series. New York. 1940.

FIELD, FREDERICK V. (editor). *Economic Handbook of the Pacific Area.* New York. 1934.

HARADA, SHUICHI. *Labor Conditions in Japan.* New York. 1928.

HAYASAKA, J. *Outline of Japanese Press.* Foreign Affairs Association of Japan. Tokyo. 1938.

HIBINO, YUTAKA. *Nippon Shindo Ron—The National Ideals of the Japanese People,* translated by A. P. McKenzie. Cambridge. 1928.

HINDMARSH, ALBERT E. *The Basis of Japanese Foreign Policy.* Cambridge, Mass. 1936.

HIRAIZUMI, KIYOSHI. *Bushido no Fukkatsu* (The Revival of Bushido). Tokyo. 1933.

HIRAO, YAGORO. *Social Policy in Japan.* Foreign Affairs Association of Japan. Tokyo. 1937.

HOLLAND, W. L. See: *Problems of the Pacific 1933,* and *1936* and *1939.*

IIZAWA, SHOJI. *Politics and Political Parties in Japan.* Foreign Affairs Association of Japan. Tokyo. 1938.

INOMATA, TSUNAO. *Nihon Noson Mondai Nyumon* (A Guide to Agrarian Problems in Japan). Tokyo. 1937.

Institute of Pacific Relations. *Japanese Data Papers.* Tokyo. 1931, 1933 and 1936.

———. *Publications on the Pacific, 1936.* New York. 1936. *Supplement.* 1938.

ISHII, RYOICHI. *Population Pressure and Economic Life in Japan.* London. 1937.

ITO, HIROBUMI. *Commentaries on the Constitution of the Empire of Japan,* translated by Ito Myoji. Tokyo. 1906.

Japan Year Book 1933. Tokyo. 1934.

Japan-Manchoukuo Year Book 1934. Tokyo. 1933.

KATAYAMA, TETSU. *Women's Movement in Japan.* Foreign Affairs Association of Japan. Tokyo. 1938.

KAZAHAYA, YASOJI. *Nippon Shakai Seisakushi* (History of Japanese Social Policy). Tokyo. 1937.

KENNEDY, CAPT. MALCOLM D. *The Problem of Japan*. London. 1936.

KIMURA, MAGOHACHIRO. *Japan's Agrarian Problems*. Foreign Affairs Association of Japan. Tokyo. 1937.

KUMAGAI, TATSUJIRO. *The Japan Young Men's Association*. Foreign Affairs Association of Japan. Tokyo. 1938.

LASKER, BRUNO. See: *Problems of the Pacific 1931* and *1933*.

LASKER, BRUNO and ROMAN, AGNES. *Propaganda from China and Japan*. New York. 1938.

MCLAREN, W. W. "Japanese Government Documents," *Transactions of the Asiatic Society of Japan*. Tokyo. 1914.

MITCHELL, KATE. See: *Problems of the Pacific 1936* and *1939*.

MITSUBISHI ECONOMIC RESEARCH BUREAU (editor). *Japanese Trade and Industry, Present and Future*. London. 1936.

MITSUI CO. LTD. (editor). *The House of Mitsui, a Record of Three Centuries*. Tokyo. 1933.

MOULTON, H. G. *Japan—An Economic and Financial Appraisal*. Washington. 1931.

NORMAN, E. H. *The Establishment of a Modern State in Japan*. I. P. R. Inquiry Series. New York. 1940.

NUGENT, DONALD R. and BELL, REGINALD. *The Pacific Area and Its Problems—A Study Guide*. New York. 1936.

ORCHARD, JOHN EWING. *Japan's Economic Position, the Progress of Industrialization*. With the collaboration of Dorothy Orchard. New York. 1930.

PENROSE, E. F. *Food Supply and Raw Materials in Japan*. Chicago. 1930.

———. *Population Theories and Their Application with Special Reference to Japan*. Stanford University. 1934.

Problems of the Pacific. 1927. Edited by J. B. Condliffe. Chicago. 1928.

———. *1929*. Edited by J. B. Condliffe. Chicago. 1930.

———. *1931*. Edited by Bruno Lasker and assisted by W. L. Holland. Chicago. 1932.

———. *1933*. Edited by Bruno Lasker and W. L. Holland. Chicago. 1934.

———. *1936*. Edited by W. L. Holland and Kate Mitchell. Chicago. 1937.

———. *1939*. Edited by Kate Mitchell and W. L. Holland. New York. 1940.

QUIGLEY, HAROLD S. *Japanese Government and Politics*. New York. 1932.

REED, JOHN PAUL. *Kokutai, a Study of Japanese Nationalism*. Mimeographed MS. University of Chicago. 1937.

REISCHAUER, ROBERT K. *Japan-Government Politics*. New York. 1939.

RUSSELL, OLAND D. *The House of Mitsui*. Boston. 1939.

SANSOM, SIR G. B. *Report on Economic and Commercial Conditions in Japan*. London. 1936.

SANSOM, G. B. and MCCRAE, H. A. *Economic Conditions in Japan to 30th June, 1928*. London. 1928.

———. *Economic Conditions in Japan 1933-34*. London. 1935.

TANIN, A. and YOHAN, E. *Militarism and Fascism in Japan*. New York. 1934.

———. *When Japan Goes to War*. New York. 1936.

TOKYO SHOSEKISHO KUMIAI, editors. *Shuppan Nenkan*, 1940. (Publications for 1940.)

UYEDA, TEIJIRO. *The Small Industries of Japan*. London. 1938.

WAR MINISTRY. *Kokubo no Hongi* (Fundamental Principles of National Defense and a Plea for Its Strengthening). Tokyo.

———. "Plege des Soldatengeistes in der Kaiserlich-Japanischen Wehrmacht," *Deutsche Gesellschaft für Natur und Völkerkunde Ostasiens*. Vol. 28. Tokyo. 1938.

WRIGHT, QUINCY. *The Existing Legal Situation As It Relates to the Conflict in the Far East*. I. P. R. Inquiry Series. New York. 1939.

YAMASHITA T. *Education in Japan*. Tokyo. 1938.

YOUNG, A. MORGAN. *Imperial Japan, 1926-1938*. New York. 1938.

———. *Japan in Recent Times, 1912-1926*. New York, 1930.

PERIODICAL ARTICLES

ABE, KENICHI. "War Conditions and the Farmer," *Contemporary Japan,* December 1938.

ALLEN, G. C. "The Concentration of Economic Control in Japan," *Economic Journal,* June 1937.

BABA, TSUNEGO. "Hostilities and Parliament," *Contemporary Japan,* March 1938.

———. "Trade Unions and the Labour Movement, *Contemporary Japan,* June 1932.

BISSON, T. A. "Origins of Sino-Japanese Hostilities," *Foreign Policy Association Reports,* March 1, 1938.

———. "The Rise of Fascism," *Foreign Policy Association Reports,* October 26, 1932.

———. "The Trend Toward Dictatorship in Japan," *Foreign Policy Association Reports,* Vol. X, No. 25.

COLEGROVE, K. S. "Japan as a Totalitarian State," *Amerasia,* March 1938.

———. "The Japanese Cabinet," *The American Political Science Review,* October 1936.

COLEGROVE, K. S. "The Japanese Foreign Office," *American Journal of International Law*, October 1936.

———. "The Japanese Constitution," *The American Political Science Review*, December 1937.

———. "The Japanese Privy Council," *The American Political Science Review*, August and November 1931.

———. "Labor Parties in Japan," *The American Political Science Review*, May 1929.

———. "Powers and Functions of the Japanese Diet," *The American Political Science Review*, December 1933, February 1934.

FARLEY, M. S. "Japan's Unsolved Tenancy Problem," *Far Eastern Survey*, July 7, 1937.

———. "War and the Japanese Budget," *Far Eastern Survey*, April 20, 1938.

———. "Electric Power Nationalized in Japan," *Far Eastern Survey*, June 15, 1938.

FISHER, GALEN M. "The Cooperative Movement in Japan," *Pacific Affairs*, December 1938.

———. "The Landlord-Peasant Struggle in Japan," *Far Eastern Survey*, September 1, 1937.

HAMADA, MICHINOSUKE. "Coping with the Agrarian Distress," *Contemporary Japan*, June 1936.

HUNSBERGER, WARREN. "Japan's Position in International Payments," *Far Eastern Survey*, June 15, 1938.

I. P. R. NOTES. (Extracts from Japanese Periodicals.) New York. 1938.

KAZAMI, AKIRA. "Whither the Japanese Peasantry?" *Contemporary Japan*, March 1934.

KOHNO, M. "The Nation Mobilizes," *Contemporary Japan*, June 1938.

MATSUKATA, S. "A Historical Study of Capitalism in Japan," *Pacific Affairs*, 1934.

MATSUO, M. "The Control of Industry in Japan," *Far Eastern Survey*, July 17, 1935.

———. "The Japanese State as Industrialist and Financier," *Far Eastern Survey*, May 25, 1936.

MIKI, KIYOSHI. "The China Affair and Japanese Thought," *Contemporary Japan*, March 1938.

MIYAGI, MINORU. "Japanese Communists' Conversion," *Contemporary Japan*, September 1933.

NAGATA, HIDEJIRO. "Japanese Faith in the Imperial Household," *Contemporary Japan*, December 1932.

OGATA, TAKETORA. "Behind Japan's Greater Cabinet," *Contemporary Japan*, December 1937.

SEKIGUCHI, YASUSHI. "The Changing Status of the Cabinet in Japan," *Pacific Affairs*, March 1938.

TANAKA, SOGORO. "The Military's Role in Japanese Politics," *Contemporary Japan*, March 1935.

WIKAWA, TADAO. "Cooperative Movement," *Contemporary Japan*, December 1932.

———. "Recent Studies in our Cooperative Movement," *Contemporary Japan*, June 1937.

YAGI, YOSHINOSUKE. "The Problem of Farm Debt Adjustment," *Kyoto University Economic Review*, July 1937.

YANAGITA, KUNIO. "Japan's Social Solidarity," *Contemporary Japan*, December 1934.

YOSHINO, SHINJI. "Our Planned Economy," *Contemporary Japan*, December 1937.

INDEX